SONY ALPHA A7CR/A7C II USER GUIDE

The Ultimate Manual to Master this Full-Frame Mirrorless Camera

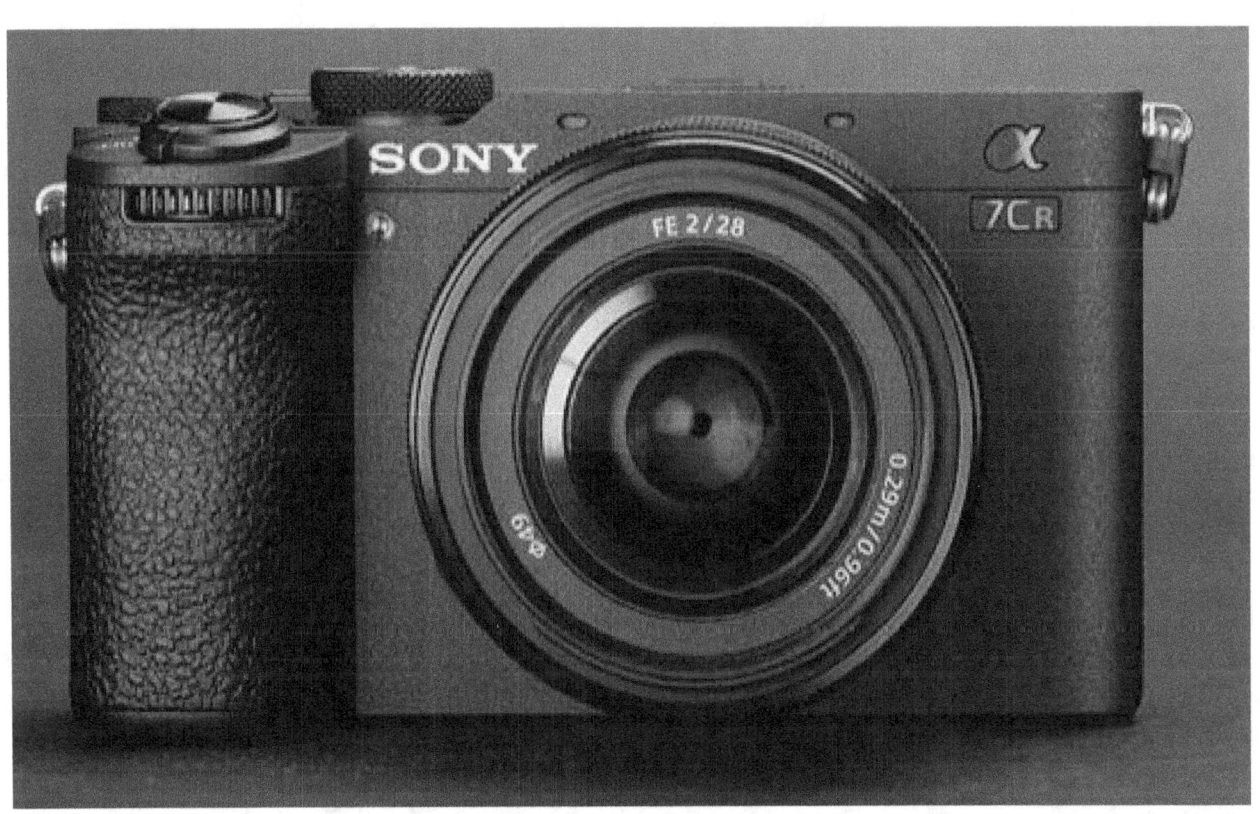

ANDERSON L. LOUIS

Copyright © 2024 Anderson L. Louis

Unauthorized reproduction, distribution, or transmission of any part of this publication in any form or by any means, including photocopying, recording, or other electronic or mechanical methods, without the prior written permission of the publisher, is prohibited.

Brief quotations may be used in critical reviews and other non-commercial uses permitted by copyright law, provided proper attribution is given.

TABLE OF CONTENTS

DISCLAIMER 4
CHAPTER ONE 6
   INTRODUCTION 6
      Overview of the Camera 6
      Comparison with Previous Models 8
CHAPTER TWO 10
   UNBOXING AND SETUP 10
      What's in the Box 10
      Inserting the Battery and Memory Card 11
      Powering On for the First Time 13
CHAPTER THREE 16
   CAMERA BODY LAYOUT AND CONTROLS 16
      Front, Rear, and Top Views of the Camera 16
      Overview of Buttons and Dials 19
      Customizable Function Buttons 22
      Using the Vari-Angle LCD Screen 24
CHAPTER FOUR 28
   GETTING STARTED: BASIC SHOOTING 28
      Selecting a Shooting Mode (Auto, Program, Manual) 28
      Adjusting Focus (Manual Focus, Autofocus) 30
      Using the Electronic Viewfinder (EVF) 32
      Basic Photography Settings (Aperture, Shutter Speed, ISO) 34
CHAPTER FIVE 36
   ADVANCED PHOTOGRAPHY FEATURES 36
      Continuous Shooting and Burst Mode 36
      Real-time Tracking Autofocus 37
      Eye AF and Face Detection 39
      Silent Shooting Mode 41
      Time-lapse Photography 43
CHAPTER SIX 46
   VIDEO RECORDING FEATURES 46
      4K Video Recording Settings 46
      Slow Motion and Quick Motion Recording 48

 Video Autofocus and Stabilization 50

 Audio Controls and External Microphone Setup 52

CHAPTER SEVEN 56

CONNECTIVITY FEATURES 56

Built-in Wi-Fi and Bluetooth Setup 56

Using Imaging Edge App for Remote Control 61

Connecting to HDMI and External Monitors 63

CHAPTER EIGHT 66

IMAGE PROCESSING AND EDITING 66

Picture Profiles and Creative Styles 66

RAW vs JPEG Shooting 68

In-Camera Image Editing Options 70

Post-Processing with Sony Imaging Software 71

CHAPTER NINE 76

LENS AND ACCESSORIES 76

Compatible E-Mount Lenses 76

Lens Adapters and Third-Party Options 79

Flash Units and External Lighting 82

Tripods, Gimbals, and Other Accessories 86

CHAPTER TEN 90

BATTERY LIFE AND POWER MANAGEMENT 90

Maximizing Battery Performance 90

Using External Battery Packs and USB Charging 91

Battery Indicator and Power Saving Tips 93

CHAPTER ELEVEN 96

MAINTENANCE AND CARE 96

Cleaning the Sensor and Lens 96

Firmware Updates and Installation 97

Troubleshooting Common Issues 99

CHAPTER TWELVE 104

CONCLUSION AND TIPS 104

Best Practices for Shooting with the A7CR/A7C II 104

Recommended Settings for Different Scenarios 105

DISCLAIMER

The contents of this book are provided for informational and entertainment purposes only. The author and publisher do not make any representations or warranties regarding the accuracy, applicability, completeness, or suitability of the contents for any purpose.

The information in this book is based on the author's personal experiences, research, and opinions, and should not be considered a substitute for professional advice. Readers are advised to consult appropriate professionals regarding their specific situations.

The author and publisher are not liable for any loss, injury, or damage allegedly arising from the information or suggestions in this book. Any reliance on such information is at the reader's own risk.

The inclusion of third-party resources, websites, or references does not imply endorsement or responsibility for their content or services.

Readers are encouraged to use their own discretion and judgment when applying the information or recommendations in this book to their own lives.

All rights reserved. No part of this book may be reproduced, distributed, or transmitted in any form or by any means without the prior written permission of the publisher, except for brief quotations in critical reviews and certain other non-commercial uses permitted by copyright law.

Thank you for reading and understanding this disclaimer.

CHAPTER ONE
INTRODUCTION

Overview of the Camera

The Sony Alpha A7CR/A7C II is a compact and versatile full-frame mirrorless camera designed for photographers and videographers who seek high performance in a portable form. Building on the success of the original A7C, the A7CR/A7C II offers several enhancements, making it ideal for travel, street, portrait, and vlogging photography.

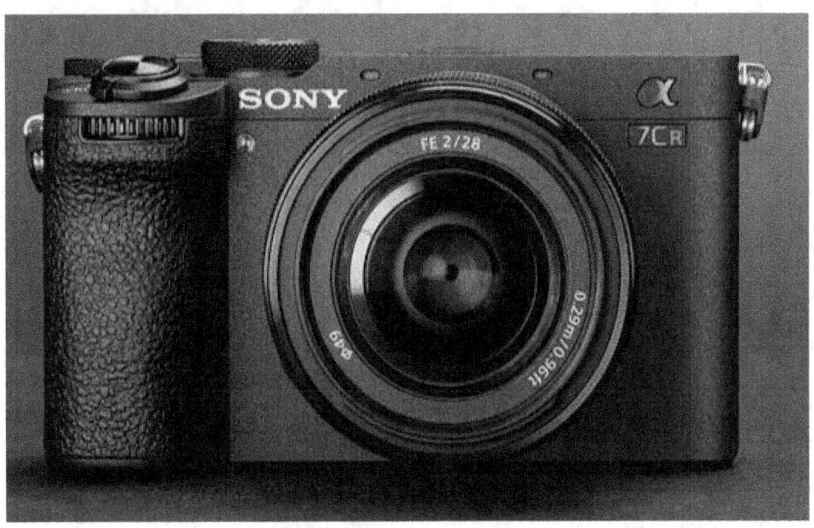

Key Features:

1. **Full-Frame 33MP Exmor R CMOS Sensor**: The A7C II is equipped with a 33MP full-frame sensor, which delivers impressive image quality, excellent dynamic range, and enhanced low-light performance. This sensor is paired with the latest BIONZ XR image processor, offering faster image processing and improved overall camera responsiveness.

2. **Compact and Lightweight Design**: The A7CR/A7C II retains the compact and lightweight form factor of the original A7C, making it one of the most portable full-frame cameras in its class. Weighing around 500g (without lens), it's designed for photographers on the go who value mobility without compromising on image quality.

3. **Advanced Autofocus System**: Sony's renowned autofocus technology is further enhanced in the A7C II, featuring **Real-time Eye AF** (for humans and animals), **Real-time Tracking**, and **759 phase-detection AF points**, covering approximately 94% of the frame. This ensures fast, accurate, and reliable focus in both still and video modes.

4. **4K Video Recording**: The A7CR/A7C II supports **4K UHD recording at 30/60fps** with full-pixel readout and no pixel binning. Additionally, it features **10-bit 4:2:2** internal recording and support for various video profiles, including **S-Log3** and **HLG**, for maximum flexibility in post-production.

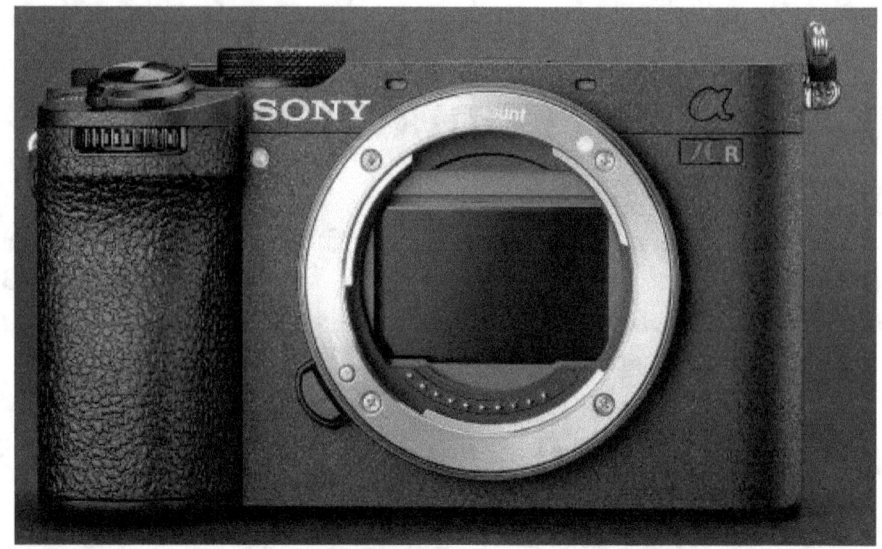

5. **5-Axis In-Body Image Stabilization (IBIS)**: The camera features 5-axis in-body stabilization that compensates for camera shake, ensuring sharper images and smoother video footage, even in challenging shooting conditions or handheld.

6. **Vari-Angle Touchscreen LCD**: A fully articulating 3.0-inch LCD touchscreen allows for easier framing, especially when shooting from difficult angles or when vlogging. The intuitive touchscreen interface provides quick access to settings and autofocus control.

7. **Enhanced Connectivity**: Built-in **Wi-Fi and Bluetooth** allow for easy sharing and remote control via the **Sony Imaging Edge app**. The camera supports fast wireless file transfer, making it convenient to share images on the go or connect to external devices.

8. **Long Battery Life and USB-C Charging**: The camera uses the high-capacity **NP-FZ100 battery**, offering extended shooting times, and supports USB-C charging, enabling power delivery from external battery packs, ensuring you're always ready to capture more.

Who is this Camera For?

The Sony Alpha A7CR/A7C II is designed for photographers and content creators who demand the flexibility of a full-frame camera but require a lightweight, compact package. It's perfect for:

- **Travel and Street Photographers** who need portability.
- **Portrait Photographers** who appreciate the eye-tracking AF and excellent image quality.
- **Vloggers and YouTubers** who need high-quality 4K video and a vari-angle screen.
- **Hybrid Shooters** who want a versatile camera for both photos and videos.

With its blend of power and portability, the A7CR/A7C II delivers professional-grade performance in a camera that's easy to carry and use in any environment.

Comparison with Previous Models

The Sony Alpha A7CR/A7C II brings significant improvements over the original Sony Alpha A7C model. Here's a detailed comparison of the two models:

Feature	Sony Alpha A7C	Sony Alpha A7CR/A7C II	Improvement
Sensor	24.2MP Full-Frame Exmor R CMOS	33MP Full-Frame Exmor R CMOS	Higher resolution for more detail
Image Processor	BIONZ X	BIONZ XR	Faster processing, improved AF, and performance
Autofocus Points	693 phase-detection AF points	759 phase-detection AF points	Expanded AF coverage, improved tracking
Autofocus Features	Real-Time Eye AF (Humans & Animals)	Real-Time Eye AF (Humans, Animals, Birds)	Enhanced Eye AF with bird support
Continuous Shooting Speed	10 fps	10 fps	Same burst rate
In-Body Image Stabilization (IBIS)	5-Axis Stabilization	5-Axis Stabilization	Same stabilization, but more refined performance
Video Resolution	4K at 30p (8-bit 4:2:0)	4K at 60p (10-bit 4:2:2)	Higher frame rate, improved color depth
Video Profiles	S-Log3, HLG	S-Log3, S-Cinetone, HLG	Added S-Cinetone for cinematic video
LCD Screen	3.0" Vari-Angle Touchscreen	3.0" Vari-Angle Touchscreen	Same size, but improved touchscreen responsiveness
Electronic Viewfinder (EVF)	2.36M-Dot EVF	2.36M-Dot EVF	Same EVF
Connectivity	Wi-Fi, Bluetooth	Wi-Fi, Bluetooth	Same connectivity, but faster data transfer
USB-C Charging	Yes	Yes	Same feature
Memory Card Slot	Single UHS-II SD Card Slot	Single UHS-II SD Card Slot	Same memory configuration
Battery Life	Approx. 740 shots (LCD)	Approx. 680 shots (LCD)	Slightly reduced due to higher processing power

Feature	Sony Alpha A7C	Sony Alpha A7CR/A7C II	Improvement
Body Design	Compact and Lightweight	Compact and Lightweight	Same form factor
Weight	509g (body only)	514g (body only)	Marginally heavier
Price	Lower, launched at a competitive price	Higher, reflecting upgraded features	Price increase for enhanced performance

Key Upgrades in Sony Alpha A7CR/A7C II:

1. **Higher Resolution Sensor**: The A7C II's 33MP sensor offers better image detail and clarity compared to the 24.2MP sensor in the original A7C, making it more suitable for high-resolution photography and cropping flexibility.

2. **BIONZ XR Processor**: The A7C II features the latest BIONZ XR image processor, which is faster and more efficient, enabling better autofocus performance, faster processing speeds, and reduced rolling shutter in video.

3. **Improved Autofocus System**: While the A7C already had an excellent autofocus system, the A7C II takes it further with **759 phase-detection AF points** and support for **Real-Time Eye AF** for birds in addition to humans and animals, offering greater flexibility for wildlife photography.

4. **Enhanced Video Capabilities**: The A7C II supports **4K 60p recording** in **10-bit 4:2:2** compared to the A7C's **4K 30p in 8-bit**. This improvement allows for smoother 4K footage with greater colour depth and dynamic range, making it a more attractive option for professional video creators.

5. **Addition of S-Cinetone**: The A7C II includes the **S-Cinetone** colour profile, which provides a more cinematic look straight out of the camera, making it easier for users to achieve high-quality video without extensive post-processing.

6. **Faster Connectivity**: While both models offer Wi-Fi and Bluetooth, the A7C II boasts faster data transfer rates for quicker image sharing and remote shooting with smartphones or tablets.

The Sony Alpha A7CR/A7C II is a notable upgrade over the original A7C, with improvements in sensor resolution, processing power, autofocus capabilities, and video performance. While it maintains the compact size and user-friendly design, the added features and enhanced specifications make it a more versatile camera for both photographers and videographers looking for a lightweight, full-frame solution.

CHAPTER TWO
UNBOXING AND SETUP

What's in the Box

When you purchase the Sony Alpha A7CR/A7C II, the following items are typically included in the box:

1. **Sony Alpha A7CR/A7C II Camera Body**: The main full-frame mirrorless camera body, featuring a compact and lightweight design.

2. **Sony NP-FZ100 Rechargeable Battery**: A high-capacity battery that provides long shooting times for both stills and video.

3. **Battery Charger (BC-QZ1)**: A dedicated charger for the NP-FZ100 battery, allowing you to charge the battery externally.

4. **USB Type-C Cable**: A USB-C cable for charging the camera directly and for connecting it to a computer or external devices for data transfer.

5. **AC Adapter**: The adapter allows for charging the camera through a power outlet when connected via the USB-C cable.

6. **Shoulder Strap**: A branded Sony shoulder strap for comfortably carrying the camera while on the go.

7. **Eyepiece Cup**: An attachable eyepiece cup for the electronic viewfinder (EVF) that enhances viewing comfort.

8. **Body Cap**: A protective cap to cover the camera's lens mount when a lens is not attached, protecting the sensor from dust and damage.

9. **User Manual**: A printed quick-start guide or manual to help you get familiar with the camera's basic functions.

10. **Warranty Documentation**: Official warranty papers for product registration and warranty service.

Optional items, depending on the seller or bundle:

- **Sony E-Mount Kit Lens** (if part of a kit): Some kits may include a **28-60mm f/4-5.6** zoom lens or other E-mount lenses, depending on the package you choose.

- **Lens Hood**: If purchasing a kit with a lens, a matching lens hood may be included for reducing flare and protecting the lens.

This complete package ensures you're ready to start shooting with the Sony Alpha A7CR/A7C II right out of the box, with all the essentials provided for charging, basic operation, and protection of the camera.

Attaching the Lens

Attaching a lens to the Sony Alpha A7CR/A7C II is simple and straightforward. Follow these steps to ensure proper attachment:

Steps for Attaching the Lens:

1. **Turn Off the Camera:** Before attaching the lens, make sure your camera is turned off to prevent any potential damage to the sensor or electrical contacts.

2. **Remove the Body Cap**: Take off the **body cap** from the camera by twisting it counterclockwise. This reveals the camera's **lens mount**.

3. **Remove the Rear Lens Cap**: Similarly, remove the **rear lens cap** from the lens you are attaching by twisting it off.

4. **Align the Mounting Indexes**: Look for the **white dot** (mounting index) on the camera's lens mount and the **white dot** on the rear of the lens. Align these two dots to ensure the lens is positioned correctly for attachment.

5. **Attach the Lens**: Once the dots are aligned, gently insert the lens into the mount. Do not apply excessive force—if aligned correctly, the lens will fit snugly into place.

6. **Twist to Lock**: Rotate the lens clockwise until you hear or feel a **click**. This ensures the lens is securely locked into place. You should not need to force it—if it doesn't click, recheck the alignment.

7. **Check the Attachment**: Gently twist the lens back and forth to ensure it's properly attached and locked. If the lens feels loose or doesn't click into place, remove it and repeat the process.

Additional Tips:
- **Avoid touching the lens mount or sensor area** to prevent dust, fingerprints, or damage.
- Use a **lens hood** (if included) for better image quality and lens protection, especially outdoors.
- Always make sure the lens clicks into place; a loose lens could cause focusing or image stabilization issues.

Once attached, you're ready to start shooting! Make sure to store your body cap and lens cap in a safe place to protect the camera and lens when not in use.

Inserting the Battery and Memory Card

To get your Sony Alpha A7CR/A7C II ready for use, you'll need to insert the battery and a memory card. Follow these simple steps:

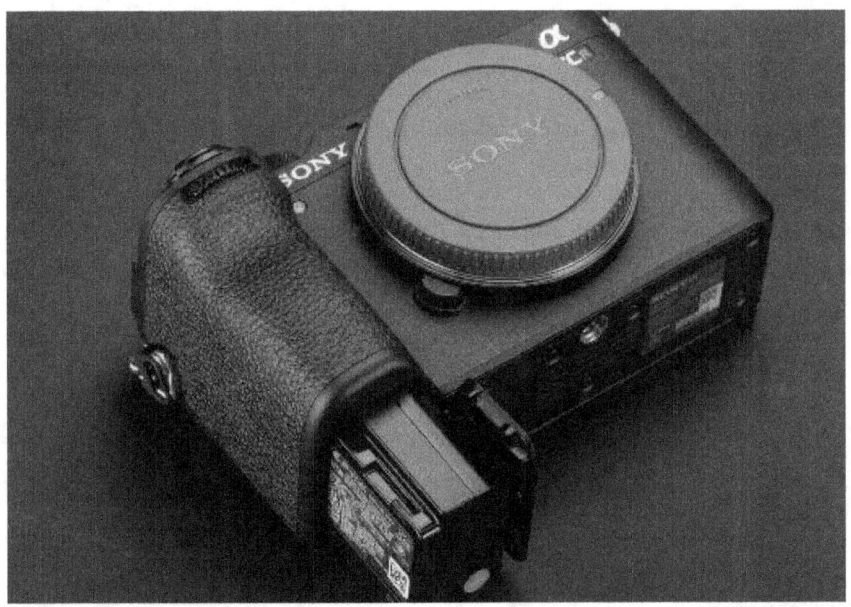

1. Inserting the Battery

a. **Locate the Battery Compartment**: The battery compartment is found on the bottom of the camera. Slide the **battery compartment cover** latch to open it.

b. **Insert the Battery**: Take the **NP-FZ100 battery** and align the contacts of the battery with the contacts in the battery compartment. Insert the battery into the compartment with the arrow pointing toward the inside. Push it in until you hear a **click** and the battery locks into place.

c. **Close the Battery Compartment**: Once the battery is securely inserted, close the battery cover and slide the latch to lock it.

Tip: Ensure the battery is fully charged before first use by charging it with the provided USB-C cable or external charger.

2. Inserting the Memory Card

a. **Locate the Memory Card Slot**: The memory card slot is also on the bottom of the camera, next to the battery compartment. Open the **memory card door** by sliding the latch.

b. **Insert the Memory Card**: Take your **SD card** (make sure it's a UHS-II card for best performance) and insert it into the memory card slot with the label facing the rear of the camera. Push the card in until it clicks into place.

c. **Close the Memory Card Door**: Once the memory card is securely inserted, close the memory card door and lock it by sliding the latch.

Note: The Sony Alpha A7CR/A7C II supports **SDXC UHS-II cards**. For faster read/write speeds, especially for 4K video, a UHS-II SD card is recommended.

3. Check Battery and Card Status

- Turn on the camera by sliding the **power switch** to the "ON" position.

- Check the **battery level indicator** and **memory card status** on the display or viewfinder to ensure both are correctly installed.

Once the battery and memory card are inserted, your camera is ready to capture images and video. Remember to format the memory card in the camera before shooting to ensure compatibility and optimal performance.

Powering On for the First Time

When you power on your Sony Alpha A7CR/A7C II for the first time, there are a few initial setup steps you need to follow. Here's how to do it:

1. Turn the Camera On

a. **Locate the Power Switch**: The **power switch** is positioned on the top right side of the camera, around the shutter button.

b. **Slide the Power Switch**: Gently slide the switch to the **"ON"** position. The camera will power up, and the LCD screen or electronic viewfinder (EVF) will activate.

2. Initial Setup Screen

Once the camera is powered on for the first time, you'll be prompted to configure some basic settings:

a. **Select Language**

- Use the **control wheel** or the touchscreen to navigate through the menu.

- Choose your preferred **language** by pressing the centre button of the control wheel or tapping the screen.

b. **Set Date and Time**

- After selecting the language, you'll be asked to set the **date, time**, and **time zone**.

- Adjust the values using the control wheel or the touchscreen, then press **OK** to confirm.

c. **Set Location Data**

- The camera may prompt you to turn on **location data acquisition** using your connected smartphone. This is useful for geotagging photos with GPS data. You can skip or enable this feature based on your preference.

3. Check Battery Level

- On the top right of the screen, you'll see the **battery indicator**. Ensure your battery has enough charge for the setup and initial use. If it's low, charge the battery using the **USB-C cable** or **battery charger** before proceeding.

4. Insert a Memory Card (If Not Done Already)

- If you haven't inserted a memory card yet, the camera may display a prompt. Insert a **UHS-II SD card** as mentioned in the previous steps, then proceed with the setup.

5. Basic Camera Setup

- The camera may provide you with a **quick setup guide** for initial settings like **image quality (JPEG/RAW), autofocus modes**, and **shooting mode**. Follow these prompts or skip them and configure settings later in the menu.

- Once the initial setup is complete, your camera is ready to use! You can start taking photos or exploring the menu for more advanced settings.

6. Optional: Format the Memory Card

- It is recommended to **format the memory card** in-camera before shooting. To do this, go to the **menu** > **Setup** > **Format** and select your memory card to erase any existing data and optimize it for use with the camera.

Now your **Sony Alpha A7CR/A7C II** is powered on, set up, and ready for shooting!

CHAPTER THREE
CAMERA BODY LAYOUT AND CONTROLS

Front, Rear, and Top Views of the Camera

Here's a breakdown of the main components visible from the front, rear, and top views of the Sony Alpha A7CR/A7C II camera:

Front View

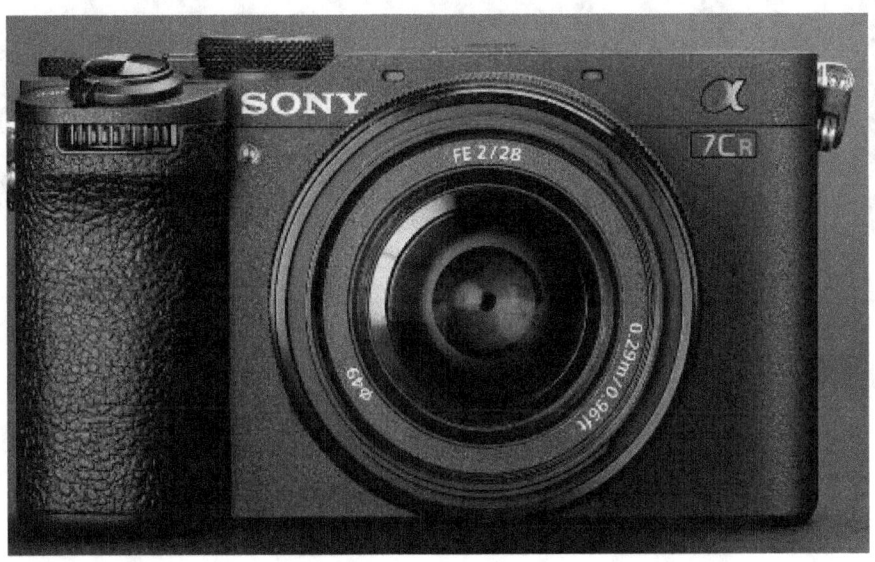

1. **Lens Mount**
   - This is the **E-mount** where you attach compatible Sony lenses.

2. **Lens Release Button**
   - Located to the right of the lens mount, this button is used to detach the lens.

3. **AF-Assist Illuminator / Self-Timer Lamp**
   - Helps with autofocus in low light and also flashes during self-timer countdown.

4. **Shutter Release Button**
   - Positioned on the top right of the grip, where your finger naturally rests, this is the main button for taking photos.

5. **Front Control Dial**
   - Located near the top of the grip, this dial allows you to adjust exposure settings like shutter speed or aperture.

6. **Grip**
   - The ergonomic grip helps provide stability when holding the camera, especially with larger lenses.

Rear View

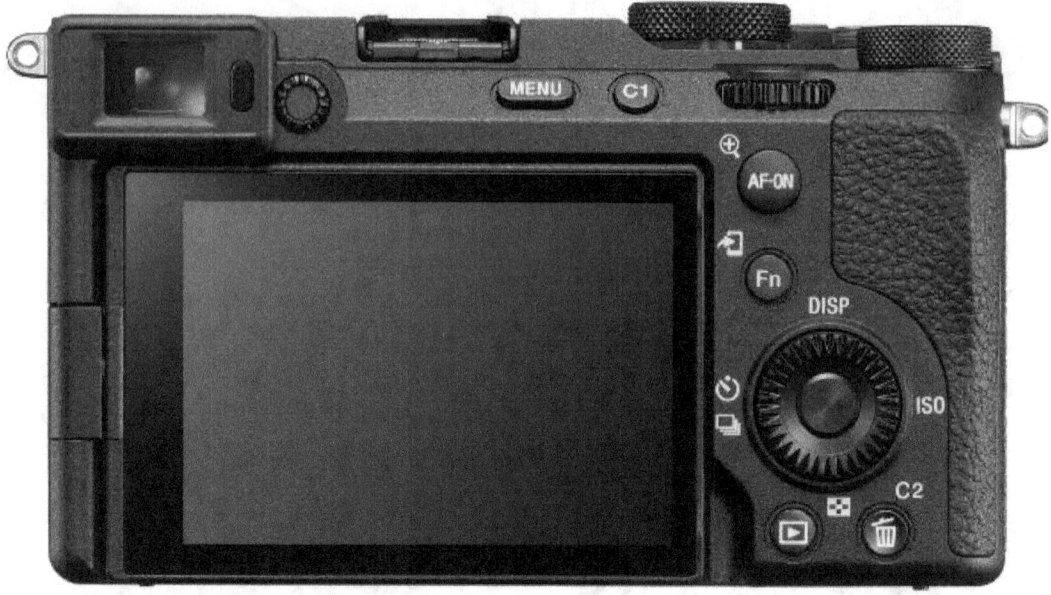

1. **Electronic Viewfinder (EVF)**
   - Located at the top centre of the rear, this 2.36M-dot EVF provides a clear preview of your shot. It can be used in bright conditions when the LCD is less visible.

2. **3.0-inch Vari-Angle LCD Touchscreen**
   - A fully articulating screen that allows you to compose shots from various angles, including vlogging, selfies, and low/high shots. The touchscreen can also be used for navigating menus and setting focus.

3. **Control Wheel / D-Pad**
   - A multifunction control for navigating menus, reviewing images, and adjusting settings such as ISO and exposure compensation.

4. **Menu Button**
   - Located on the top-left side of the rear, this button gives access to the camera's menu for settings and configurations.

5. **Fn (Function) Button**
   - Provides quick access to a customizable set of frequently used settings like white balance, focus mode, and drive mode.

6. **Playback Button**
   - Located below the control wheel, this button lets you view and manage images and videos you've captured.

7. **AF-ON Button**
   - A dedicated button for activating autofocus while shooting, often used for back-button focusing.

8. **AEL (Auto Exposure Lock) Button**
    - Locks exposure settings while recomposing the shot.

9. **Customizable C1 and C2 Buttons**
    - These buttons can be assigned to various functions for quick access, allowing you to customize the camera to your workflow.

10. **Movie Recording Button**
    - A dedicated button for starting and stopping video recording, located conveniently next to the EVF for easy access.

Top View
1. **Mode Dial**
    - This large dial allows you to switch between various shooting modes, such as **Manual (M)**, **Aperture Priority (A)**, **Shutter Priority (S)**, **Program Auto (P)**, and custom modes like video and scene selections.

2. **Exposure Compensation Dial**
    - This dial enables easy adjustment of exposure compensation for brightening or darkening the image in real-time.

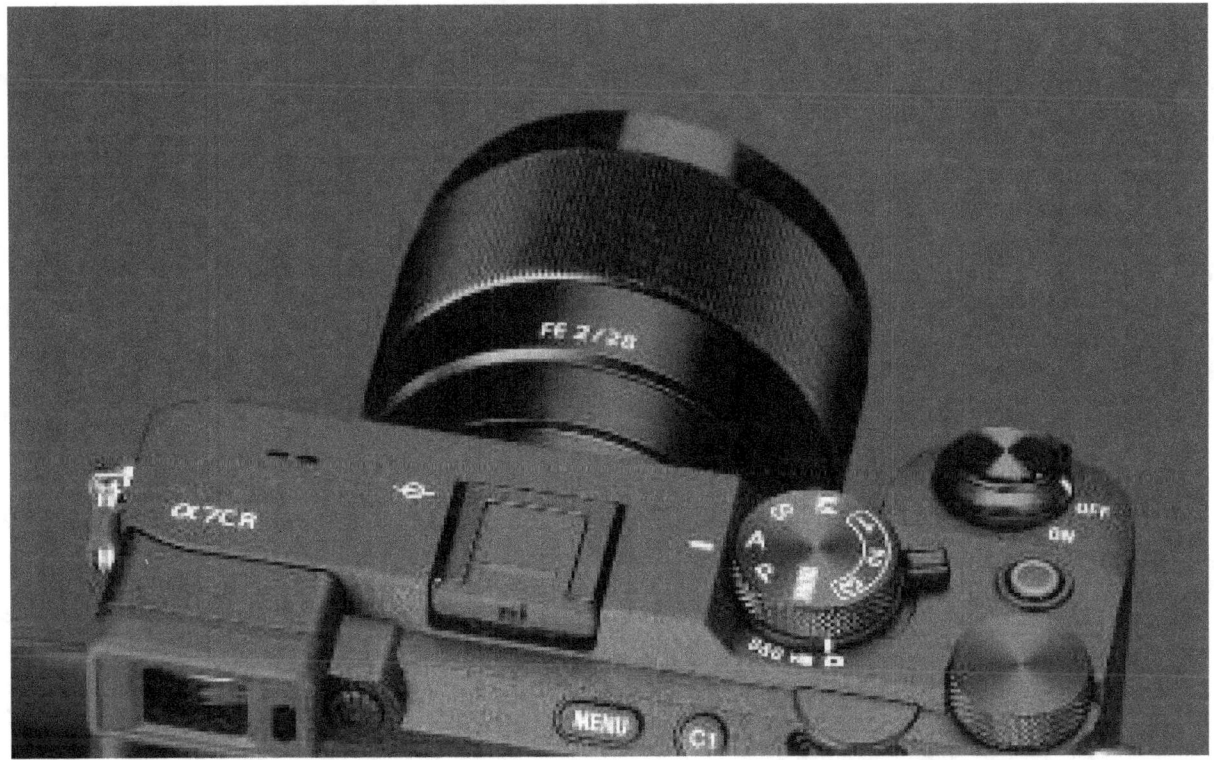

3. **Front Control Dial**
    - Used to adjust exposure settings such as aperture or shutter speed, depending on the mode selected.

4. **Hot Shoe / Multi-Interface Shoe**
    - The **hot shoe** allows you to attach external accessories like flashes, microphones, or other Sony accessories.

5. **Built-in Stereo Microphone**
    - Positioned near the hot shoe, this microphone is used for in-camera audio recording.

6. **Power Switch**
    - Wrapped around the shutter button, this switch is used to power the camera on or off.

7. **Movie Recording Button**
    - A dedicated button for starting/stopping video recording (as also mentioned in the rear view).

These views give you a good understanding of the physical layout and functionality of the Sony Alpha A7CR/A7C II, allowing for intuitive handling and efficient access to its features

Overview of Buttons and Dials

The Sony Alpha A7CR/A7C II is equipped with several buttons and dials that provide quick access to important functions and settings, allowing you to customize and control the camera with case. Here's an overview of the key buttons and dials on this full-frame mirrorless camera:

Top of the Camera
1. **Mode Dial**
    - Located on the top right, this is the main dial to switch between different shooting modes. Common modes include:
        - **Manual (M)**: Full control over both aperture and shutter speed.
        - **Aperture Priority (A)**: You control the aperture, and the camera sets the shutter speed.
        - **Shutter Priority (S)**: You control the shutter speed, and the camera sets the aperture.
        - **Program Auto (P)**: The camera sets both aperture and shutter speed, but you can still tweak other settings.
        - **Custom (C1, C2, C3)**: User-defined modes for quick access to frequently used settings.
        - **Video Mode**: Optimized for recording videos with quick access to video-specific settings.

2. **Exposure Compensation Dial**

- Found next to the mode dial, this dial allows you to quickly adjust exposure compensation (making the image brighter or darker) in most automatic and semi-automatic modes.

3. **Front Control Dial**
    - Positioned in front of the shutter button, this dial is used to adjust primary exposure settings such as shutter speed in manual mode, or aperture in aperture priority mode.

4. **Movie Record Button**
    - Located on the top of the camera near the viewfinder, this button is dedicated to starting and stopping video recording.

5. **Shutter Button**
    - Wrapped by the power switch, this button is used to capture photos. A half-press activates autofocus, while a full press takes the picture.

6. **Power Switch**
    - Located around the shutter button, this switch is used to turn the camera on and off.

7. **Multi-Interface Hot Shoe**
    - Positioned at the centre-top of the camera, this is used to attach external accessories such as flashes, microphones, or wireless transmitters.

Rear of the Camera
1. **Electronic Viewfinder (EVF)**
    - This high-resolution viewfinder gives a live preview of your shot and displays important settings like exposure and focus.

2. **3.0-inch Vari-Angle LCD Touchscreen**
    - Fully articulating screen that allows you to control the camera using touch inputs. You can swipe through menus, set focus, and review images.

3. **AF-ON Button**
    - Located near the EVF, this button is used to activate autofocus independently of the shutter button, ideal for back-button focusing.

4. **AEL (Auto Exposure Lock) Button**
    - This button locks the exposure while recomposing, ensuring the light reading remains consistent.

5. **Control Wheel (D-Pad)**
    - A versatile dial used for navigating through menus and settings. The directional buttons can be customized to perform specific tasks (e.g., adjusting ISO, white balance, or drive mode).

- **Up Button**: Often assigned to ISO settings.
- **Left Button**: Typically assigned to drive mode (single, continuous, self-timer).
- **Right Button**: Often assigned to white balance adjustments.
- **Down Button**: Customizable for various functions.
- **Centre Button**: Confirms selections in menus or focuses in certain shooting modes.

6. **Fn (Function) Button**
    - This button opens a customizable quick-access menu where you can adjust frequently used settings such as focus mode, white balance, and metering.

7. **Playback Button**
    - Located below the control wheel, this button is used to review photos and videos you've already captured.

8. **Menu Button**
    - Positioned on the top left of the rear, the menu button opens the full camera menu where you can access and adjust all camera settings.

9. **C1 and C2 Custom Buttons**
    - These buttons, located near the shutter and on the rear, are fully customizable and can be assigned to frequently used settings such as ISO, white balance, or focus mode.

Front of the Camera
1. **Lens Release Button**
    - Located on the right side of the lens mount, this button is pressed to unlock and remove the lens.

2. **Front Control Dial**
    - On the front of the camera grip, this dial is used to adjust exposure settings such as aperture and shutter speed, depending on the selected shooting mode.

3. **Focus Mode Selector**
    - Found near the lens mount, this button or switch toggles between different autofocus modes (AF-S, AF-C, DMF, or manual focus).

Side of the Camera
1. **USB Type-C and HDMI Ports**
    - These ports allow for charging, data transfer, and video output to external devices.

2. **Memory Card Slot**

o Located on the side panel, this is where you insert SD cards for photo and video storage.

3. **Microphone and Headphone Jacks**

    o Ports for connecting external microphones and headphones to monitor and improve audio quality during video recording.

The buttons and dials on the Sony Alpha A7CR/A7C II are thoughtfully arranged for intuitive control, allowing both novice and professional photographers to make quick adjustments without diving into menus. Custom buttons (C1, C2) and the function button (Fn) can be tailored to your shooting style, providing flexibility and efficiency in handling the camera.

Customizable Function Buttons

The Sony Alpha A7CR/A7C II provides several customizable buttons that allow you to assign frequently used functions for quick access. These buttons can greatly enhance your shooting efficiency by providing direct access to the settings you use most often.

Here's a guide to the key customizable function buttons:

1. C1 and C2 Buttons (Custom Buttons)

These buttons are located on the top and rear of the camera and are designed for user customization. You can assign different functions to these buttons based on your preferences.

- **C1 Button**: Usually positioned near the **shutter button**, this is often used for quick access to settings such as **ISO**, **white balance**, or **focus area**.

- **C2 Button**: Located near the **AF-ON** button on the rear of the camera, this is typically assigned to settings like **metering mode**, **focus mode**, or **drive mode**.

Common Assignable Functions:

- **Focus Mode** (AF-S, AF-C, DMF, MF)
- **ISO Sensitivity**
- **White Balance**
- **Focus Area** (Wide, Zone, Centre, Flexible Spot)
- **Drive Mode** (Single, Continuous, Bracketing)
- **Metering Mode** (Multi, Spot, Centre)
- **Face/Eye Priority in AF**
- **Picture Profiles** (useful for video recording)

2. Fn (Function) Button

The **Fn button** gives you access to a customizable quick-access menu. When pressed, it opens a menu with up to 12 settings that you can assign, making it a powerful tool for fast adjustments without diving into the full camera menu.

- **Default Location**: Located on the rear of the camera, below the **control wheel**.
- **How to Customize**:
    - Press the **Menu** button.
    - Navigate to the **Custom Operation** section.
    - Select **Function Menu Set**.
    - Here you can assign different functions to the slots available in the **Fn Menu**.

Common Assignable Functions in Fn Menu:

- **Focus Mode/Area**
- **Drive Mode**
- **Picture Profile**
- **Creative Style** (for picture customization)
- **Focus Magnifier** (useful for manual focus)
- **APS-C/Super 35mm Mode**
- **Steady Shot** (image stabilization)

3. AF-ON Button

The **AF-ON** button is typically used for back-button focusing, allowing you to decouple autofocus from the shutter button. This provides greater control over focusing, especially for action or portrait photography.

- **Default Location**: On the rear of the camera near the **thumb grip**.
- **How to Customize**:
    - Go to the **Custom Operation** settings in the **Menu**.
    - Choose **AF-ON Button** and assign different autofocus-related functions such as **Eye AF** or **Focus Lock**.

4. AEL Button (Auto Exposure Lock)

The **AEL button** locks the exposure when pressed, allowing you to recompose the shot without changing the exposure settings. However, it can be customized to perform other functions such as toggling focus modes or even acting as a secondary AF button.

- **Default Location**: Near the **AF-ON** button on the rear of the camera.
- **How to Customize**:
    - Navigate to the **Custom Operation** settings.

o Choose the **AEL Button** function and assign the desired operation, such as **Focus Mode**, **Focus Area**, or **Eye AF**.

5. Control Wheel (D-Pad)

Each direction on the **control wheel** (up, down, left, right) can be customized to provide direct access to specific settings. This can be incredibly useful for frequently adjusted parameters like ISO, white balance, or drive mode.

- **Default Assignments** (customizable):
    - **Up**: ISO adjustment.
    - **Left**: Drive mode (single, continuous, timer).
    - **Right**: White balance.
    - **Down**: Often assigned to focus mode or other settings.
- **How to Customize**:
    - Go to the **Menu** > **Custom Operation** > **Custom Key**.
    - Select the **Control Wheel** and customize each directional button.

How to Customize Function Buttons

1. **Press the Menu Button**
    - Navigate to the **Camera Settings** or **Setup Menu**.
2. **Go to the Custom Operation Menu**
    - Under the **Custom Operation** tab, select **Custom Key** to customize the function buttons.
3. **Assign Functions to the Desired Buttons**
    - Select the button you want to customize (C1, C2, Fn, etc.) and assign your preferred function from the list of available options.
4. **Confirm and Test**
    - After assigning the functions, press the buttons during shooting to test if the customization works as intended.

The customizable buttons on the Sony Alpha A7CR/A7C II allow for a highly personalized shooting experience. Whether you're a photographer or videographer, customizing these buttons to your workflow can save time and make accessing your most-used settings fast and efficient. Take the time to experiment with different configurations to see what works best for you!

Using the Vari-Angle LCD Screen

The Vari-Angle LCD touchscreen on the Sony Alpha A7CR/A7C II provides flexibility and versatility, allowing you to shoot from various angles while maintaining a clear view of your composition. Here's a guide to making the most of this articulating screen:

1. Fully Articulating Design

The **Vari-Angle LCD screen** can be pulled out and rotated to enable shooting from challenging perspectives. Here's how you can use it:

- **Tilting Up or Down**:
  - The screen tilts **up to 180°** for high-angle shots (e.g., shooting over a crowd).
  - It can also tilt **downward** for low-angle shots (e.g., for ground-level or macro photography).

- **Side Rotation**:
  - The screen rotates **horizontally**, making it perfect for **selfies**, **vlogging**, or **video recording** when the camera is facing you.
  - You can position the screen at various angles to compose shots when using a tripod or in handheld situations where the viewfinder is less practical.

2. Touchscreen Functionality

The LCD is not just a display but also a fully functional **touchscreen**. Here are some key touch features:

- **Touch Focus**: Tap anywhere on the screen to set the focus point quickly. This is particularly useful for fast-moving subjects or when recomposing a shot.

- **Touch Shutter**: You can enable the **Touch Shutter** feature, which allows you to take a picture simply by tapping the screen. This can be useful for discreet shooting or when using the camera on a tripod.

- **Menu Navigation**: Navigate through the camera's menus and settings using touch. This makes adjusting parameters like **ISO, white balance**, and **focus modes** quick and intuitive.

- **Playback Controls**: Swipe through photos and videos during playback. You can also pinch to zoom in on images to check sharpness and detail or swipe down to delete an image.

3. Shooting from Different Angles

The Vari-Angle LCD allows you to get creative with your compositions. Here are some examples of how you can use it for various shooting styles:

- **High-Angle Shots**:
  - When shooting over obstacles or crowds, flip the screen **upward** so you can see the live preview while holding the camera above your head.

- **Low-Angle Shots**:
  - For ground-level shots, flip the screen **downward** so you don't have to crouch or lie on the ground to compose the shot.

- **Self-Portraits/Vlogging**:

- For selfies or vlogging, flip the screen out to the **side** and rotate it to face you. This ensures you can monitor your composition and ensure proper framing while recording yourself.

- **Macro Photography**:
    - For extreme close-ups, the screen can be tilted to help you get precise focus without physically straining to look through the viewfinder.

4. Using the Screen in Bright Conditions

When shooting in **bright sunlight** or reflective conditions, the LCD screen may become difficult to view. Here are a few tips:

- **Increase Screen Brightness**: Adjust the brightness of the LCD screen through the **Menu > Display Settings** to make the screen easier to see in bright conditions.

- **Use the Viewfinder**: When the screen is difficult to view, switch to the **Electronic Viewfinder (EVF)** for clearer composition.

- **Anti-Reflective Coating**: The screen has an anti-reflective coating to reduce glare, but you may still need to adjust your position or use the viewfinder in extreme lighting situations.

5. Protecting the LCD Screen

The articulating screen can be rotated to face **inward** (toward the body of the camera) when not in use. This helps protect it from scratches, smudges, or accidental damage during transport or storage.

The Vari-Angle LCD touchscreen on the Sony Alpha A7CR/A7C II enhances versatility and creativity by allowing you to compose shots from any angle, whether you're shooting stills or videos. The touchscreen features make navigating the camera's settings faster and more intuitive, giving you greater control and efficiency while working in different shooting environments.

CHAPTER FOUR
GETTING STARTED: BASIC SHOOTING
Selecting a Shooting Mode (Auto, Program, Manual)

The Sony Alpha A7CR/A7C II offers various shooting modes to cater to different photography needs and skill levels. Understanding how to select and use these modes is crucial for maximizing the camera's capabilities. Here's a detailed guide on the three primary shooting modes: Auto, Program, and Manual.

1. Auto Mode

Auto Mode is ideal for beginners or when you want to capture images quickly without delving into complex settings. In this mode, the camera automatically adjusts exposure, focus, and other settings to ensure a well-exposed image.

- **How to Select Auto Mode**:
    1. **Locate the Mode Dial** on the top of the camera.
    2. Turn the dial to the **Auto** setting, typically marked with a green camera icon or labelled as "Auto."

- **Key Features**:
    - **Automatic Exposure**: The camera calculates the optimal shutter speed, aperture, and ISO based on the lighting conditions.
    - **Automatic Focus**: The camera uses its autofocus system to find and lock onto the subject.
    - **Ease of Use**: Great for casual shooting, family events, or when you need to focus on composition without worrying about technical settings.

- **Limitations**:
    - Limited creative control over exposure settings.
    - May not perform well in low-light situations or with fast-moving subjects.

2. Program Mode (P)

Program Mode is a step up from Auto Mode, allowing you to retain some control over the camera's settings while still benefiting from automatic exposure calculations. In this mode, you can adjust various settings and access advanced features.

- **How to Select Program Mode**:
    1. **Turn the Mode Dial** to **P** (Program) mode.

- **Key Features**:
    - **Programmed Exposure**: The camera selects a combination of shutter speed and aperture for proper exposure, but you can change either setting without affecting exposure.
    - **Flexible Control**: Use the **Front Control Dial** to adjust the exposure settings while maintaining the same exposure level.
    - **Access to Camera Functions**: You can use the **Fn button** or touch the LCD to access other settings like ISO, white balance, and drive mode.
- **Benefits**:
    - Offers more flexibility compared to Auto Mode.
    - Ideal for situations where you want quick adjustments while maintaining creative control over the image.
- **Limitations**:
    - Less creative control than Manual Mode, as the camera still calculates exposure settings.

3. Manual Mode (M)

Manual Mode provides full control over all exposure settings, allowing you to set the shutter speed, aperture, and ISO independently. This mode is best suited for experienced photographers who want complete creative control.

- **How to Select Manual Mode**:
    1. **Turn the Mode Dial** to **M** (Manual) mode.
- **Key Features**:
    - **Full Control**: You manually set the shutter speed, aperture, and ISO for complete creative flexibility.
    - **Exposure Metering**: The camera displays an exposure meter in the viewfinder or LCD, helping you adjust settings for proper exposure.
    - **Creative Control**: You can experiment with depth of field, motion blur, and other creative effects.
- **Benefits**:
    - Ideal for advanced techniques like long exposures, shallow depth of field, or specific lighting conditions.
    - Allows for precise adjustments and creative expression.

- **Considerations**:
    - Requires understanding of exposure principles (shutter speed, aperture, ISO) and practice to master.
    - Can be challenging for beginners or in rapidly changing lighting situations.

Selecting the right shooting mode on the **Sony Alpha A7CR/A7C II** is crucial for achieving your desired photographic results. **Auto Mode** is perfect for quick and easy shooting, **Program Mode** offers flexibility with some control, and **Manual Mode** gives you complete creative power. Familiarizing yourself with these modes and when to use each will help you make the most of your camera and enhance your photography skills.

Adjusting Focus (Manual Focus, Autofocus)

The Sony Alpha A7CR/A7C II offers advanced focusing options that cater to various shooting scenarios, whether you prefer manual control or rely on the camera's autofocus system. Here's a comprehensive guide to adjusting focus using both Manual Focus and Autofocus modes.

1. Autofocus (AF)

Autofocus is a convenient feature that allows the camera to automatically determine the best focus point based on the subject. The A7CR/A7C II has multiple autofocus modes and settings to enhance your shooting experience.

Types of Autofocus:

- **Single-shot AF (AF-S)**:
    - Locks focus when the shutter button is half-pressed. Ideal for stationary subjects.
- **Continuous AF (AF-C)**:
    - Continuously adjusts focus on moving subjects, making it suitable for action photography.
- **Direct Manual Focus (DMF)**:
    - Combines autofocus with manual adjustments. The camera initially focuses automatically, allowing you to fine-tune focus manually afterward.

How to Enable Autofocus:

1. **Press the Menu Button**.
2. Navigate to **Camera Settings > Focus Mode**.
3. Choose your preferred autofocus mode (AF-S, AF-C, or DMF).

Setting Focus Area: The A7CR/A7C II allows you to select different focus areas based on your subject:

- **Wide**: The camera uses a broad area for focusing, suitable for general shooting.

- **Zone**: Focuses on a specific area within the frame, which is helpful for tracking subjects in a particular zone.
- **Centre**: Focuses on the centre of the frame, useful for portraits or subjects in the middle of the scene.
- **Flexible Spot**: Lets you choose a specific point to focus on, giving you greater control over composition.

How to Set Focus Area:

1. Press the **Fn** button to bring up the Function Menu.
2. Select **Focus Area** and choose your desired setting using the control wheel.

2. Manual Focus (MF)

Manual Focus gives you complete control over the focus point, allowing for precise adjustments, especially in challenging lighting conditions or intricate compositions.

How to Enable Manual Focus:

1. **Press the Menu Button**.
2. Navigate to **Camera Settings** > **Focus Mode**.
3. Select **Manual Focus (MF)**.

Adjusting Focus Manually:

- **Focus Ring**: Rotate the focus ring on the lens to adjust the focus.
- **Focus Peaking**: This feature highlights in-focus areas with colour overlays, making it easier to see what's in focus.

How to Activate Focus Peaking:

1. Press the **Menu Button**.
2. Go to **Camera Settings** > **Peaking Level** and set it to **Low**, **Mid**, or **High** based on your preference.
3. Choose a colour (Red, Yellow, or White) for the peaking indicator.

Using Magnification for Precise Focus: You can magnify the image on the LCD or viewfinder for accurate manual focusing.

How to Magnify:

1. In **MF mode**, press the **C1 button** (or customize a button for this function).
2. Use the **control wheel** to zoom in or out, adjusting the magnification to focus accurately on your subject.

The **Sony Alpha A7CR/A7C II** provides flexible focusing options to suit your shooting style. **Autofocus** offers convenience and speed for dynamic subjects, while **Manual Focus** grants precision and control, especially in challenging conditions. By mastering these focus modes, you can enhance your photography and capture the images you envision.

Using the Electronic Viewfinder (EVF)

The Electronic Viewfinder (EVF) on the Sony Alpha A7CR/A7C II is a powerful feature that provides a clear, real-time display of your composition and camera settings, allowing for precise control over your shooting experience. Here's how to effectively use the EVF and maximize its capabilities.

1. Activating the EVF

The EVF automatically activates when you bring the camera to your eye, thanks to its built-in proximity sensor. If it doesn't activate, you can manually turn it on:

- **How to Turn On the EVF**:
    1. Press the **Menu Button**.
    2. Navigate to **Display/Auto Review** settings.
    3. Ensure that the **Viewfinder/Monitor** setting is set to **Auto** or manually select **Viewfinder**.

2. Adjusting EVF Settings

You can customize various settings on the EVF to improve your shooting experience:

- **Brightness and Contrast**:
    - Navigate to **Menu > Display/Auto Review > EVF Settings**.
    - Adjust the **Brightness** and **Contrast** to suit your viewing preference and lighting conditions.

- **Colour Settings**:
    - Choose between different colour settings to make the display easier to read in various lighting environments.

- **Frame Rate**:
    - Select a higher frame rate for smoother motion, especially useful for tracking fast-moving subjects.

3. Utilizing EVF Features

The EVF provides several useful features to enhance your shooting capabilities:

- **Real-Time Exposure Preview**:
    - The EVF displays real-time adjustments to exposure settings (shutter speed, aperture, ISO), allowing you to see how changes will affect the final image before capturing it.

- **Focus Peaking**:
    - If you're using manual focus, enabling **Focus Peaking** will highlight in-focus areas in the EVF, making it easier to achieve sharp focus.
- **Zebra Patterns**:
    - Use the **Zebra Pattern** feature to indicate overexposed areas in the EVF. This helps ensure that highlights are not blown out, allowing for better exposure control.
- **Grid Display**:
    - Activate a grid overlay in the EVF to help with composition and aligning your shots according to the rule of thirds or other compositional techniques.

4. Adjusting the Diopter

To ensure a clear view through the EVF, you may need to adjust the diopter setting based on your vision:

- **How to Adjust the Diopter**:
    1. Locate the **diopter adjustment dial** next to the EVF.
    2. Look through the EVF while adjusting the dial until the view is sharp and clear.

5. Switching Between EVF and LCD Screen

The A7CR/A7C II allows you to easily switch between the EVF and the LCD screen for different shooting scenarios:

- **Automatic Switching**:
    - The camera should automatically switch between the EVF and LCD based on proximity (using the proximity sensor).
- **Manual Switching**:
    - If you want to force a switch, you can do so through the **Menu** under **Display/Auto Review** settings, selecting either **Viewfinder** or **Monitor**.

6. Using the EVF for Video Recording

The EVF can also be beneficial when recording videos, particularly in bright conditions where the LCD may be difficult to see:

- **How to Use the EVF for Video**:
    - Simply bring the camera to your eye to use the EVF as you would for still photography.
    - Ensure that the camera is set to **Video Mode**, and you can adjust settings as needed while viewing through the EVF.

The **Electronic Viewfinder (EVF)** on the **Sony Alpha A7CR/A7C II** enhances your shooting experience by providing a clear, real-time view of your composition and settings. By familiarizing yourself with its features and settings, you can improve your precision and creativity, whether you're capturing stills or recording video. The EVF is a valuable tool for achieving the best possible results in various shooting conditions.

Basic Photography Settings (Aperture, Shutter Speed, ISO)

Understanding the basic photography settings—Aperture, Shutter Speed, and ISO—is essential for mastering exposure and achieving your desired creative effects. Here's a detailed guide on these three fundamental components and how to adjust them on the Sony Alpha A7CR/A7C II.

1. Aperture

Aperture refers to the size of the opening in the lens through which light passes. It is measured in **f-stops** (e.g., f/2.8, f/4, f/5.6), with smaller numbers representing larger openings that allow more light in.

- **Effects of Aperture**:
    - **Depth of Field**: A larger aperture (smaller f-stop number) results in a shallow depth of field, blurring the background and isolating the subject (great for portraits). A smaller aperture (larger f-stop number) increases depth of field, keeping more of the scene in focus (ideal for landscapes).
    - **Exposure**: A larger aperture lets in more light, affecting the exposure of your image.
- **How to Adjust Aperture**:

1. Turn the **Mode Dial** to **A** (Aperture Priority) or **M** (Manual) mode.

2. Use the **control dial** to adjust the aperture value. Rotate it to see the f-stop values change on the LCD or EVF.

2. Shutter Speed

Shutter Speed refers to the duration the camera's shutter remains open, allowing light to hit the sensor. It is measured in seconds or fractions of a second (e.g., 1/1000s, 1/60s, 2s).

- **Effects of Shutter Speed**:
    - **Motion Blur**: A fast shutter speed (e.g., 1/1000s) freezes motion, making it perfect for action shots or sports photography. A slow shutter speed (e.g., 1/30s) captures motion blur, which can convey a sense of movement in your images (ideal for waterfalls or light trails).
    - **Exposure**: A slower shutter speed lets in more light, affecting the overall exposure of the image.
- **How to Adjust Shutter Speed**:

1. Turn the **Mode Dial** to **S** (Shutter Priority) or **M** (Manual) mode.

2.   Use the **control dial** to change the shutter speed value, observing the changes on the LCD or EVF.

3. ISO

ISO measures the sensitivity of the camera's sensor to light. A lower ISO (e.g., 100 or 200) is less sensitive to light and is ideal for bright conditions, while a higher ISO (e.g., 1600 or 3200) increases sensitivity, allowing you to shoot in low-light conditions.

- **Effects of ISO**:
    - **Noise**: Increasing the ISO can introduce digital noise or grain in your images, especially at very high settings. It's best to use the lowest ISO possible for the cleanest image quality.
    - **Exposure**: Higher ISO settings enable shooting in lower light but may compromise image quality.
- **How to Adjust ISO**:

1.   Press the **ISO button** (usually marked with "ISO") on the camera or navigate through the **Menu**.

2.   Use the **control wheel** or arrow keys to select your desired ISO value.

3.   In **Auto ISO** mode, you can set a maximum ISO limit to maintain better image quality in low-light conditions.

Putting It All Together

The **exposure triangle** consists of aperture, shutter speed, and ISO, which work together to determine the exposure of your images:

- **Aperture** affects depth of field and light entry.
- **Shutter Speed** controls motion blur and light entry duration.
- **ISO** adjusts sensor sensitivity to light.

When adjusting these settings, consider the following:

- **Balancing Exposure**: If you adjust one setting, you may need to compensate with the others to maintain proper exposure.
- **Creative Intent**: Think about the effect you want to achieve. For example, if you want to blur the background, use a wide aperture; if you want to freeze motion, use a fast shutter speed.

Mastering **Aperture**, **Shutter Speed**, and **ISO** is crucial for achieving desired exposure and creative effects in your photography. The **Sony Alpha A7CR/A7C II** provides easy access to adjust these settings, allowing you to experiment and capture stunning images in various conditions. By understanding how these elements interact, you can take your photography to the next level.

CHAPTER FIVE
ADVANCED PHOTOGRAPHY FEATURES

Continuous Shooting and Burst Mode

Continuous Shooting and Burst Mode are essential features on the Sony Alpha A7CR/A7C II that allow photographers to capture a series of images in rapid succession. These modes are particularly useful for photographing fast-moving subjects, action scenes, or capturing fleeting moments. Here's a comprehensive guide on how to use these features effectively.

1. Understanding Continuous Shooting and Burst Mode

- **Continuous Shooting**: This mode enables the camera to take multiple shots in quick succession as long as the shutter button is pressed. It's beneficial for capturing fast action or when you want to ensure you don't miss a critical moment.

- **Burst Mode**: Often referred to as "High-Speed Continuous Shooting," this is a specific setting that allows for shooting at a faster frame rate, capturing more images per second.

2. Setting Up Continuous Shooting

How to Enable Continuous Shooting:

1. **Turn the Mode Dial** to your desired shooting mode (e.g., Aperture Priority, Shutter Priority, or Manual).

2. Press the **Menu Button**.

3. Navigate to **Camera Settings** > **Drive Mode**.

4. Select **Continuous Shooting** or **Burst Mode**.

Types of Continuous Shooting Modes:

- **Low Speed**: Captures images at a slower frame rate (e.g., 3-5 frames per second).

- **High Speed**: Captures images at a faster frame rate (e.g., 10-20 frames per second), depending on the camera settings and conditions.

- **Silent Shooting**: Uses electronic shutter for silent shooting, beneficial in quiet environments.

3. Customizing Continuous Shooting Settings

You can customize several settings to optimize your continuous shooting experience:

- **Focus Mode**:
    - For tracking moving subjects, set the camera to **Continuous Autofocus (AF-C)**. This ensures the camera continuously adjusts focus as the subject moves.

- **Exposure Mode**:

- o Choose between **Auto Exposure (AE)** or **Manual Exposure (ME)**. AE will automatically adjust settings, while ME allows you to maintain consistent exposure across all shots.
- **Image Quality**:
  - o Ensure you have the appropriate image quality selected (JPEG or RAW). Note that RAW files take up more space and may reduce the maximum frame rate in burst mode.

4. Using Continuous Shooting Effectively

Here are some tips for making the most of continuous shooting and burst mode:

- **Hold Steady**: Keep the camera steady while pressing the shutter button. Consider using a tripod or stabilizer for better results, especially at slower shutter speeds.
- **Use the Right Lens**: Lenses with faster autofocus capabilities and image stabilization can enhance the effectiveness of continuous shooting, especially for action shots.
- **Monitor Buffer Limit**: The camera has a buffer limit, which determines how many images can be taken in rapid succession before the camera slows down. Check the specifications for your camera to understand this limit and plan accordingly.
- **Practice Timing**: For sports or wildlife photography, anticipate action and press the shutter button slightly before the peak moment to ensure you capture the shot.

5. Reviewing Burst Mode Images

After capturing images in burst mode, you can review them in the camera's playback mode. Here's how:

1. Press the **Playback Button** to view your images.
2. Use the **control wheel** or arrow keys to navigate through the captured burst images.
3. You can rate or delete unwanted shots to manage storage space effectively.

Continuous Shooting and **Burst Mode** on the **Sony Alpha A7CR/A7C II** provide photographers with powerful tools for capturing dynamic scenes and fast-moving subjects. By understanding how to set up and customize these features, as well as practicing effective techniques, you can significantly enhance your photography and ensure you capture the perfect moment every time.

Real-time Tracking Autofocus

Real-Time Tracking Autofocus is one of the standout features of the Sony Alpha A7CR/A7C II, designed to provide precise and reliable focus on moving subjects. This advanced autofocus system utilizes AI-driven algorithms to keep your subjects in sharp focus, making it ideal for sports, wildlife, and dynamic shooting environments. Here's a detailed guide on how to utilize this feature effectively.

1. Understanding Real-Time Tracking Autofocus

Real-Time Tracking Autofocus employs advanced subject recognition technology to track subjects across the frame, allowing for smooth and accurate focusing. The system identifies and locks onto subjects, even as they move, ensuring they remain in focus throughout your shots.

Key Features:

- **AI-Based Detection**: The camera uses deep learning technology to recognize faces, eyes, and other subjects.

- **Wide Tracking Area**: The autofocus system covers a broad area of the frame, allowing for flexibility in composition.

- **Responsive Tracking**: The camera continuously adjusts focus as subjects move, making it easier to capture fast action without losing sharpness.

2. Activating Real-Time Tracking Autofocus

To enable Real-Time Tracking Autofocus, follow these steps:

1. **Turn the Mode Dial** to your desired shooting mode (e.g., Aperture Priority, Shutter Priority, or Manual).
2. Press the **Menu Button**.
3. Navigate to **Camera Settings** > **Focus Mode**.
4. Select **Real-Time Tracking** from the autofocus options.

3. Using Real-Time Tracking Autofocus

Once Real-Time Tracking Autofocus is enabled, you can begin using it to capture your subjects effectively:

- **Selecting Your Subject**:
    - **Touch Screen**: If your camera model features a touch screen, you can tap on the subject you want to focus on directly from the LCD. This action will activate Real-Time Tracking.
    - **Control Wheel**: If not using touch, use the control wheel or joystick to select your subject in the viewfinder or on the LCD screen.

- **Half-Pressing the Shutter Button**:
    - Once you've selected your subject, half-press the shutter button. The camera will lock onto the subject, and you'll see a tracking box around it in the viewfinder or on the LCD screen.

- **Maintaining Focus**:
    - As the subject moves, the camera will automatically adjust focus to keep the subject sharp. Ensure you keep the selected subject within the frame to maintain tracking.

4. Customizing Real-Time Tracking Settings
You can tailor the Real-Time Tracking Autofocus settings to suit your shooting style:

- **AF Area Settings**:
    - Navigate to **Menu > Camera Settings > AF Area**. Here, you can choose different area settings that may work better for your shooting conditions, such as **Wide** or **Flexible Spot**.

- **Subject Detection**:
    - In some cases, you may want to prioritize detecting specific subjects (e.g., animals or people). Set the subject detection to focus on either **Human** or **Animal** in the menu.

5. Tips for Effective Use of Real-Time Tracking
- **Lighting Conditions**: Ensure you are shooting in adequate lighting conditions, as low light can affect the performance of the autofocus system.

- **Movement**: For moving subjects, try to anticipate their path and be prepared to adjust the framing to keep them within the tracking area.

- **Combination with Other Modes**: You can use Real-Time Tracking in conjunction with other autofocus modes, such as **Continuous Autofocus (AF-C)**, for more flexibility.

- **Test and Experiment**: Take some time to practice with different subjects and settings to understand how the autofocus system responds in various scenarios.

Real-Time Tracking Autofocus on the **Sony Alpha A7CR/A7C II** offers photographers a powerful tool for capturing fast-moving subjects with precision and ease. By understanding how to activate and use this feature, along with its customization options, you can enhance your photography skills and ensure that your subjects are always in focus, no matter how dynamic the shooting environment.

Eye AF and Face Detection

Eye AF (Autofocus) and Face Detection are advanced autofocus features on the Sony Alpha A7CR/A7C II that enhance portrait photography and other scenarios where subject recognition is critical.

These features ensure that the eyes and faces of your subjects remain in sharp focus, providing you with stunning and professional-looking images. Here's a detailed guide on how to utilize these features effectively.

1. Understanding Eye AF and Face Detection
- **Eye AF**: This feature specifically targets the eyes of a subject, locking focus on the eye to ensure it is sharp and clear. This is particularly useful in portrait photography, where having the eyes in focus is crucial.

- **Face Detection**: This function detects and recognizes faces within the frame, allowing the camera to prioritize focus on the faces of people in your composition. It works in conjunction with Eye AF to enhance focus accuracy on the subject's eyes.

2. Activating Eye AF and Face Detection

To enable Eye AF and Face Detection, follow these steps:

1. **Turn the Mode Dial** to your desired shooting mode (e.g., Aperture Priority, Shutter Priority, or Manual).
2. Press the **Menu Button**.
3. Navigate to **Camera Settings** > **AF (Autofocus)** > **Face/Eye Detection**.
4. Enable **Face Detection** and set **Eye AF** to the desired subject (Human or Animal).

3. Using Eye AF

Once Eye AF is activated, follow these steps to effectively utilize the feature:

- **Selecting the Subject**:
    - Aim the camera at your subject, ensuring their face is within the frame.
    - You can use the **Control Wheel** or **Joystick** to select the eye you want to focus on. The camera will automatically detect and track the eye.
- **Half-Pressing the Shutter Button**:
    - Half-press the shutter button to lock focus on the selected eye. You'll see a green box appear around the eye, indicating that it is in focus.
- **Continuous Tracking**:
    - As your subject moves, the camera will continuously track the eye as long as you keep the shutter button half-pressed.

4. Using Face Detection

Face Detection works seamlessly with Eye AF but can also be used independently:

- **Detecting Faces**:
    - When you frame your shot, the camera will automatically detect any faces present. The focus will prioritize these faces, ensuring they are sharp in the image.
- **Multiple Faces**:
    - If multiple faces are detected, you can choose which face to focus on by touching the desired face on the LCD screen or using the joystick.

5. Customizing Eye AF and Face Detection Settings

You can customize these settings for optimal performance:

- **AF Area Settings**:

- Navigate to **Menu > Camera Settings > AF Area** to adjust the AF area mode (e.g., Wide, Zone, or Flexible Spot) depending on your shooting scenario.

- **Priority Settings**:
  - You can prioritize either **Eye AF** or **Face Detection** based on your shooting style. This can be adjusted in the menu under **AF Settings**.

6. Tips for Effective Use of Eye AF and Face Detection

- **Lighting Conditions**: Ensure that your subject's face is well-lit, as low-light conditions may hinder the camera's ability to detect faces and eyes.

- **Shooting Angle**: Position yourself at the subject's eye level for the best results with Eye AF. This angle often leads to more engaging portraits.

- **Use with Continuous Autofocus (AF-C)**: Combine Eye AF with AF-C mode to keep tracking the subject as they move.

- **Experiment with Different Subjects**: Test Eye AF and Face Detection with various subjects and settings to understand how the system performs under different conditions.

Eye AF and Face Detection on the Sony Alpha A7CR/A7C II are powerful tools that significantly enhance portrait photography and other scenarios where focus accuracy is essential. By activating and effectively using these features, you can ensure your subjects are always in sharp focus, allowing for beautiful, professional-quality images that truly capture the moment.

Silent Shooting Mode

Silent Shooting Mode is a key feature of the Sony Alpha A7CR/A7C II, allowing photographers to capture images without the mechanical sounds typically associated with taking a photo. This feature is particularly useful in environments where silence is crucial, such as during weddings, performances, or wildlife photography. Here's a comprehensive guide on how to utilize Silent Shooting Mode effectively.

1. Understanding Silent Shooting Mode

Silent Shooting Mode operates by using the camera's **electronic shutter**, which eliminates the noise produced by the mechanical shutter. This allows for completely silent operation while still capturing high-quality images.

Key Benefits:

- **Discreet Shooting**: Ideal for capturing candid moments without disturbing subjects.

- **Vibration-Free**: The electronic shutter eliminates vibrations associated with mechanical shutters, leading to potentially sharper images, especially at slower shutter speeds.

- **High-Speed Shooting**: In some scenarios, electronic shutters can enable faster shutter speeds compared to mechanical shutters.

2. Activating Silent Shooting Mode

To enable Silent Shooting Mode on the Sony Alpha A7CR/A7C II, follow these steps:

1. **Turn the Mode Dial** to your desired shooting mode (e.g., Aperture Priority, Shutter Priority, or Manual).
2. Press the **Menu Button**.
3. Navigate to **Camera Settings** > **Shutter/Steady Shot**.
4. Select **Silent Shooting** and toggle it to **On**.

Alternatively, you can customize a function button to quickly enable or disable Silent Shooting Mode for more convenience.

3. Using Silent Shooting Mode

Once Silent Shooting Mode is activated, you can start taking photos quietly:

- **Compose Your Shot**: Frame your subject as you would in regular shooting.
- **Focus**: Use your preferred autofocus method to lock focus on your subject.
- **Capture the Image**: Press the shutter button to take the photo without the typical shutter sound.

Important Consideration: When using Silent Shooting Mode, be mindful that some functions, such as flash and certain autofocus modes, may be limited or unavailable.

4. Customizing Silent Shooting Settings

You can adjust various settings to optimize your experience in Silent Shooting Mode:

- **Exposure Settings**: Ensure your exposure settings (shutter speed, aperture, and ISO) are set appropriately, as the electronic shutter may behave differently than the mechanical shutter, especially at extreme settings.
- **Continuous Shooting**: Silent Shooting Mode can be used in continuous shooting (burst) mode. Make sure to adjust the drive mode to continuous if you plan to take multiple shots in quick succession.
- **Image Quality**: Consider shooting in RAW format for better post-processing flexibility, as this format retains more image data compared to JPEG.

5. Tips for Effective Use of Silent Shooting Mode

- **Monitor Lighting Conditions**: While Silent Shooting is effective in various lighting situations, ensure that your camera's settings are suitable for the light available to avoid underexposed or overexposed images.

- **Practice with Different Subjects**: Test Silent Shooting Mode with different subjects, including fast-moving or unpredictable subjects, to understand how the electronic shutter performs in various scenarios.

- **Use a Tripod or Stabilization**: If shooting at slower shutter speeds, using a tripod or stabilization can help prevent motion blur, as the absence of a mechanical shutter can sometimes lead to slight vibrations.

Silent Shooting Mode on the Sony Alpha A7CR/A7C II provides photographers with the ability to capture images discreetly, making it an invaluable tool for various shooting scenarios. By understanding how to activate and utilize this feature effectively, you can enhance your photography experience and capture moments without disturbing your subjects. Whether you're in a quiet environment or simply prefer a silent shooting experience, this mode allows for greater creative freedom.

Time-lapse Photography

Time-lapse photography is a creative technique that involves capturing a series of images at set intervals to create a video that shows the passage of time in a condensed format. The Sony Alpha A7CR/A7C II offers features that make it easy to experiment with and produce stunning time-lapse sequences. Here's a comprehensive guide on how to set up and execute time-lapse photography using this camera.

1. Understanding Time-Lapse Photography

Time-lapse photography captures changes over time by taking multiple photos at specified intervals. When played back at a faster frame rate, these images create a video that showcases movements that are too slow to see in real-time, such as the movement of clouds, flowers blooming, or cityscapes.

Key Elements:

- **Interval**: The time between each shot.

- **Duration**: The total length of the time-lapse, which will dictate how many frames you need to capture.

- **Playback Speed**: The speed at which the captured frames are played back, affecting the final video length.

2. Setting Up Time-Lapse Photography

To create a time-lapse sequence with the Sony Alpha A7CR/A7C II, follow these steps:

1. **Mount the Camera**: Secure your camera on a sturdy tripod to avoid movement between shots.

2. **Turn the Mode Dial**: Set it to **Manual (M)** mode to have full control over your exposure settings.

3. **Adjust Settings**:
    - **ISO**: Set an appropriate ISO for your lighting conditions.

- **Aperture**: Choose a suitable aperture for depth of field.
- **Shutter Speed**: Adjust the shutter speed, keeping in mind that slower speeds may require a longer interval between shots to avoid motion blur.

4. **Enable Time-Lapse**:
   - Press the **Menu Button**.
   - Navigate to **Camera Settings** > **Interval Shooting**.
   - Set the **Shooting Interval** (the time between shots).
   - Set the **Number of Shots** (how many frames you want to capture).

5. **Select a Shooting Mode**: Choose **Continuous Shooting** or **Single Shooting** mode, depending on your preference.

3. Using the Time-Lapse Feature

Once your camera is set up, you can start capturing your time-lapse:

- **Start Shooting**: Press the shutter button or use a remote trigger to start capturing your time-lapse sequence.
- **Monitor the Scene**: Keep an eye on the scene and lighting conditions throughout the capture. Adjust settings, if necessary, especially if the lighting changes significantly.

4. Post-Processing Time-Lapse Images

After capturing your time-lapse sequence, you may need to process the images:

- **Editing Software**: Use software like Adobe Premiere Pro, Final Cut Pro, or specialized time-lapse software to compile your images into a video.
- **Frame Rate**: Decide on the playback frame rate (e.g., 24 or 30 frames per second) to determine how smooth your final video will be.
- **Transitions and Effects**: Add transitions, effects, or colour corrections to enhance your final video.

5. Tips for Successful Time-Lapse Photography

- **Plan Your Shoot**: Scout locations in advance and plan the timing of your shoot, especially if shooting natural phenomena (like sunsets or sunrises).
- **Use an ND Filter**: In bright conditions, a Neutral Density (ND) filter can help control exposure while allowing you to use slower shutter speeds for smoother motion.

- **Keep Battery Life in Mind**: Time-lapse shooting can drain your battery quickly, so ensure you have a fully charged battery and consider using an external power source if capturing for an extended period.
- **Experiment with Intervals**: Different subjects may require different intervals for the best effect. Experiment with various settings to find what works best for your specific scene.

Time-lapse photography with the Sony Alpha A7CR/A7C II opens up a world of creative possibilities. By understanding how to set up and execute time-lapse sequences effectively, you can capture stunning visual stories that reveal the beauty of movement and change over time. Whether you're shooting urban landscapes, natural phenomena, or everyday activities, time-lapse can add a dynamic element to your photography portfolio.

CHAPTER SIX
VIDEO RECORDING FEATURES

4K Video Recording Settings

The Sony Alpha A7CR/A7C II offers advanced 4K video recording capabilities, allowing filmmakers and videographers to capture stunning high-resolution footage with remarkable detail. Understanding how to configure the video settings is crucial for maximizing the camera's performance and achieving professional-quality results. Here's a comprehensive guide on setting up 4K video recording on your camera.

1. Overview of 4K Video Recording

4K video refers to a resolution of 3840 x 2160 pixels, which is four times the resolution of Full HD (1920 x 1080). This high resolution allows for more detail and clarity, making it ideal for cinematic projects, vlogs, and other video content.

Key Features:

- **High Bitrate**: 4K recording can utilize high bitrates, enhancing video quality.
- **Multiple Frame Rates**: The camera supports various frame rates for creative control, including 24p, 30p, and 60p.
- **S-Log and HDR**: The A7CR/A7C II supports S-Log profiles and HDR recording, providing greater dynamic range and flexibility in post-production.

2. Configuring 4K Video Recording Settings

To set up 4K video recording on your Sony Alpha A7CR/A7C II, follow these steps:

1. **Turn the Mode Dial**: Set the mode dial to **Video (Movie)** mode.
2. **Access the Menu**: Press the **Menu Button**.
3. **Navigate to Video Settings**:
    - Go to **Camera Settings** > **Video Settings** or **Movie Settings**.
4. **Select 4K Resolution**:
    - Look for the **Record Settings** or **File Format** option.
    - Choose **XAVC S 4K** for high-quality 4K recording.
5. **Set Frame Rate**:
    - In the **Record Settings**, select your desired frame rate (e.g., 24p, 30p, or 60p) based on your project needs.
    - For cinematic footage, 24p is commonly used, while 30p or 60p may be better for action or fast-moving scenes.

6. **Bitrate Settings**:
   - Choose a higher bitrate (e.g., 100 Mbps or 200 Mbps) for better image quality. Higher bitrates capture more detail but result in larger file sizes.

7. **S-Log and Picture Profiles** (optional):
   - For advanced colour grading, you can enable **S-Log3** or **S-Log2**. Navigate to **Picture Profile** and select your preferred S-Log option.
   - Adjust the **Gamma** and **Colour Mode** settings based on your desired look.

8. **Audio Settings**:
   - Navigate to the **Audio Settings** section to set the audio input, volume levels, and monitor audio through headphones if necessary.

3. Recording 4K Video

Once you have configured the settings, you can start recording 4K video:

- **Compose Your Shot**: Frame your subject and check focus before starting the recording.
- **Press the Record Button**: Use the dedicated movie record button to start and stop recording.
- **Monitor Exposure and Focus**: Keep an eye on your exposure settings, especially if shooting in changing lighting conditions. Use manual focus if necessary for precision.

4. Tips for Successful 4K Video Recording

- **Use a Tripod or Stabilizer**: For steady shots, consider using a tripod, gimbal, or stabilizer to minimize camera shake.
- **Check Storage**: 4K video files can be large, so ensure you have ample storage space on your memory card. Use high-speed SD cards that support UHS-II for optimal performance.
- **Monitor Temperature**: Extended recording times can cause the camera to heat up. Keep an eye on the temperature and be prepared to take breaks if necessary.
- **Lighting**: Proper lighting is essential for high-quality video. Consider using external lights or reflectors to achieve the desired effect.
- **Experiment with Angles and Techniques**: Don't hesitate to try different camera angles, movements, and techniques to enhance your video's visual storytelling.

The Sony Alpha A7CR/A7C II is equipped with powerful 4K video recording capabilities that can elevate your filmmaking projects. By understanding how to configure the settings effectively, you can capture stunning, high-resolution footage that meets professional standards.

Whether you're shooting short films, vlogs, or creative projects, mastering 4K video recording will significantly enhance your videography skills.

Slow Motion and Quick Motion Recording

The Sony Alpha A7CR/A7C II offers versatile recording options, including slow motion and quick motion (also known as time-lapse) video capabilities. These features allow you to create dynamic visual effects that can enhance storytelling in your video projects. Here's a detailed guide on how to set up and use these recording modes effectively.

1. Slow Motion Recording

Slow motion recording captures video at a higher frame rate and plays it back at a standard frame rate, resulting in smooth, dramatic slow-motion footage.

Key Features:

- **High Frame Rates**: You can record at frame rates such as 120p or 240p, allowing for ultra-slow motion when played back at 24p or 30p.
- **Increased Detail**: Higher frame rates capture more detail in fast-moving subjects.

Setting Up Slow Motion Recording

To configure slow motion recording on your Sony Alpha A7CR/A7C II, follow these steps:

1. **Turn the Mode Dial**: Set the camera to **Video (Movie)** mode.
2. **Access the Menu**: Press the **Menu Button**.
3. **Navigate to Video Settings**:
   - Go to **Camera Settings** > **Video Settings** or **Movie Settings**.
4. **Select Slow Motion Settings**:
   - Look for the **Record Settings** or **File Format** option.
   - Choose **XAVC S HD** for higher frame rates (as 4K recording may limit frame rates).
5. **Set Frame Rate**:
   - Choose a frame rate like **120p** or **240p** for slow motion.
   - Ensure your project settings (e.g., 24p or 30p) are compatible with the frame rate chosen for playback.
6. **Adjust Other Settings**:
   - Set the resolution and bitrate as needed. Higher bitrates may enhance quality but increase file size.
7. **Monitor Audio**: If you need audio, note that high frame rates may limit audio recording capabilities.

Recording Slow Motion Video

- **Compose Your Shot**: Frame your subject appropriately and check focus.
- **Press the Record Button**: Start recording by pressing the dedicated movie record button.

- **Focus on Fast Movement**: Slow motion is particularly effective for fast actions, such as sports, dance, or nature.

2. Quick Motion (Time-Lapse) Recording

Quick motion recording (time-lapse) involves capturing a series of images at set intervals, which are then played back at a standard frame rate to show the passage of time quickly.

Key Features:

- **Interval Shooting**: Capture photos at specified intervals (e.g., every 1 second) over a period of time.
- **Compressed Time**: This technique condenses hours or days into a short video, revealing changes not visible in real time.

Setting Up Quick Motion (Time-Lapse) Recording

To set up quick motion recording, follow these steps:

1. **Turn the Mode Dial**: Set the camera to **Video (Movie)** mode.
2. **Access the Menu**: Press the **Menu Button**.
3. **Navigate to Interval Shooting**:
    - Go to **Camera Settings** > **Interval Shooting** or **Time-Lapse** settings.
4. **Set the Shooting Interval**:
    - Determine how frequently you want the camera to take a shot (e.g., every 1, 2, or 5 seconds).
5. **Choose the Number of Shots**:
    - Decide how many frames you want to capture for your time-lapse sequence.
6. **Select Video Output Settings**:
    - Go to **Movie Settings** to select the desired resolution and frame rate for the final output (e.g., 4K or Full HD at 24p or 30p).
7. **Start Recording**:
    - After settings are configured, press the record button to begin capturing your time-lapse sequence.

3. Tips for Effective Slow Motion and Quick Motion Recording

- **Lighting**: Ensure good lighting conditions for both recording types. Slow motion may require more light due to higher shutter speeds, while time-lapse may need consistent lighting over the recording duration.
- **Stability**: Use a tripod for stable shots, especially for time-lapse and slow-motion footage.

- **Plan Your Shots**: For time-lapse, consider the changes in the scene you wish to capture and plan your intervals accordingly.
- **Experiment with Settings**: Don't hesitate to try different frame rates and intervals to see how they affect the final output. Adjust your settings based on the subject and desired effect.

The **Sony Alpha A7CR/A7C II** provides powerful options for both **slow motion** and **quick motion** recording. By understanding how to configure these settings and utilizing the camera's capabilities, you can create visually captivating content that enhances your storytelling. Whether you're aiming for dramatic slow-motion effects or showcasing the beauty of time passing, mastering these techniques will elevate your video projects.

Video Autofocus and Stabilization

The **Sony Alpha A7CR/A7C II** is equipped with advanced video autofocus (AF) and stabilization features, making it an excellent choice for videographers seeking to capture smooth and sharp footage. Understanding how to utilize these capabilities effectively can significantly enhance the quality of your video recordings. Here's a detailed guide on video autofocus and stabilization settings.

1. Video Autofocus

Video Autofocus ensures that your subject remains in focus during recording, even if they move within the frame. The A7CR/A7C II features several autofocus technologies that enhance its performance in video shooting.

Key Features:

- **Fast Hybrid AF**: Combines phase detection and contrast detection for quick and accurate focusing.
- **Real-Time Eye AF**: Automatically detects and focuses on the eyes of subjects, making it ideal for portrait and documentary filming.
- **Face Detection**: Identifies and tracks faces in the frame, keeping them in sharp focus.

Setting Up Video Autofocus

To configure the autofocus settings for video recording, follow these steps:

1. **Turn the Mode Dial**: Set the camera to **Video (Movie)** mode.
2. **Access the Menu**: Press the **Menu Button**.
3. **Navigate to Autofocus Settings**:
   - Go to **Camera Settings** > **AF/MF** settings or **AF Settings**.
4. **Select Autofocus Mode**:
   - Choose **Continuous AF (AF-C)** for video, ensuring that the camera continuously adjusts focus during recording.
5. **Enable Eye AF** (if applicable):

- Navigate to **Face/Eye AF** settings and enable **Real-Time Eye AF** to ensure the camera automatically focuses on the subject's eyes.

6. **Set Focus Area**:
    - Choose a focus area that suits your shooting style. Options include **Wide**, **Centre**, or **Flexible Spot**.

2. Video Stabilization

Video Stabilization is crucial for achieving smooth footage, especially when shooting handheld or during motion. The A7CR/A7C II incorporates several stabilization features to minimize camera shake.

Key Features:

- **In-Body Image Stabilization (IBIS)**: The camera features a 5-axis stabilization system that compensates for various types of movement.
- **Active Mode Stabilization**: Provides enhanced stabilization, particularly effective for walking or moving shots.

Setting Up Video Stabilization

To enable and configure stabilization settings, follow these steps:

1. **Access the Menu**: Press the **Menu Button**.
2. **Navigate to Stabilization Settings**:
    - Go to **Camera Settings** > **Stabilization Settings**.
3. **Enable Steady Shot**:
    - Turn on **Steady Shot** to activate in-body stabilization.
4. **Select Active Mode** (optional):
    - For increased stabilization during video recording, enable **Active Mode**. This is especially useful for handheld shooting or when moving.

3. Tips for Effective Autofocus and Stabilization in Video

- **Plan Your Shots**: Anticipate movement in your scene and adjust focus settings accordingly. Use **Wide AF** for general shots and **Flexible Spot** for more precise control.
- **Use a Tripod for Stability**: While IBIS is effective, using a tripod or gimbal can further enhance stability, especially for static shots.
- **Monitor Focus During Recording**: Use the camera's monitoring features, such as focus peaking, to ensure your subject remains in focus during shooting.
- **Test Your Settings**: Before your main shoot, test autofocus and stabilization settings to ensure they perform well in your specific environment and lighting conditions.

- **Consider Lighting**: Autofocus performance can be affected by low-light conditions. Ensure sufficient lighting or adjust your settings to enhance AF performance.

The Sony Alpha A7CR/A7C II offers advanced video autofocus and stabilization features that significantly enhance the quality of your recordings. By configuring these settings correctly and understanding how to use them effectively, you can create smooth, sharp, and professional-looking videos. Whether you're shooting interviews, action scenes, or vlogs, mastering these capabilities will elevate your videography skills and ensure captivating content.

Audio Controls and External Microphone Setup

Good audio quality is crucial for video production, and the Sony Alpha A7CR/A7C II provides robust audio controls and options for using external microphones. This guide will help you navigate the audio settings, set up external microphones, and optimize your audio recording for high-quality sound.

1. Overview of Audio Controls

The A7CR/A7C II comes equipped with various audio controls that allow you to adjust recording levels, monitor audio, and choose between different input options.

Key Features:

- **Built-in Microphone**: The camera features a built-in stereo microphone for basic audio capture.

- **Audio Input Options**: A 3.5mm microphone input allows for external microphone connections.

- **Audio Level Control**: You can manually adjust audio levels to prevent distortion and ensure optimal sound quality.

- **Wind Noise Reduction**: This feature helps reduce wind noise during outdoor recordings.

Accessing Audio Controls

To access and adjust audio controls, follow these steps:

1. **Turn the Mode Dial**: Set the camera to **Video (Movie)** mode.

2. **Access the Menu**: Press the **Menu Button**.

3. **Navigate to Audio Settings**:
   - Go to **Audio Settings** or **Sound Settings** within the camera menu.

4. **Adjust Audio Levels**:
   - Look for the **Audio Level Display**. Use the **Audio Level Control** option to adjust recording levels. Aim for a level that peaks around -12dB to -6dB to avoid distortion.

5. **Enable Wind Noise Reduction** (if applicable):
   - Activate the **Wind Noise Reduction** feature in the audio settings when shooting outdoors.

2. Setting Up an External Microphone

Using an external microphone can significantly improve audio quality, especially for interviews, vlogs, or any situation where clear audio is essential.

Connecting an External Microphone

1. **Choose Your Microphone**: Select a compatible external microphone, such as a shotgun, lavalier, or handheld microphone.

2. **Connect the Microphone**:
   - Plug the microphone's 3.5mm connector into the **microphone input** on the camera.

3. **Access the Audio Settings**:
   - Repeat the steps to access the **Audio Settings** menu.

4. **Select Input Source**:
   - Check that the camera recognizes the external microphone. You may see options to select the input source, ensuring it is set to the external microphone.

5. **Adjust Audio Levels**:
   - Use the audio level controls to adjust the input level based on your microphone's sensitivity. Monitor the audio levels to ensure they are within the ideal range.

3. Monitoring Audio

Monitoring audio while recording is essential to ensure quality sound capture.

Using Headphones:

- Connect a pair of headphones to the **headphone output** jack on the camera.
- This allows you to monitor audio in real-time and catch any issues during recording.

Adjusting Headphone Volume:

- Access the audio settings to adjust the headphone volume level, ensuring you can hear the audio clearly without distortion.

4. Tips for Optimal Audio Recording

- **Test Your Setup**: Before your main shoot, do a quick test recording with your external microphone to ensure everything is working properly.

- **Position Your Microphone**: Pay attention to the microphone placement. For interviews, keep the microphone close to the subject for clearer sound.

- **Use a Windshield**: If recording outdoors, consider using a windscreen on your external microphone to reduce wind noise.

- **Check Battery Levels**: If using battery-powered external microphones, ensure they are charged or have fresh batteries.
- **Record Ambient Sound**: Capture a few seconds of ambient sound at the beginning of your recording. This can be useful for post-production audio editing.

The Sony Alpha A7CR/A7C II provides comprehensive audio controls and options for external microphone setup, allowing you to achieve high-quality sound for your video projects. By understanding the audio settings, using external microphones effectively, and monitoring audio levels, you can enhance your video production quality. With the right audio setup, your videos will not only look great but also sound professional.

3. **Consult the Manual**: Refer to the user manual for specific error messages and suggested solutions.

Most common issues with the **Sony Alpha A7CR/A7C II** can be resolved with simple troubleshooting steps. By following this guide, users can quickly diagnose and rectify problems, ensuring a seamless photography and videography experience. If problems persist despite troubleshooting, contacting Sony customer support or a professional technician may be necessary for further assistance.

1. **Adjust Settings**: Reduce screen brightness, disable Wi-Fi/Bluetooth when not in use, and turn off image review.

2. **Use Airplane Mode**: When not using wireless features, switch the camera to airplane mode to conserve battery life.

3. **Monitor Battery Health**: If the battery drains quickly even after adjustments, it may be time to replace the battery.

6. Poor Image Quality or Artifacts
Possible Causes:

- Incorrect camera settings or lens issues.

Troubleshooting Steps:

1. **Check Settings**: Ensure you are shooting in the appropriate mode (e.g., RAW or JPEG) and that all settings (aperture, ISO, etc.) are correct for the environment.

2. **Inspect Lens**: Check for any scratches or damage to the lens, which could affect image quality. Clean the lens if necessary.

7. Audio Issues in Video Recording
Possible Causes:

- Incorrect audio settings or external microphone issues.

Troubleshooting Steps:

1. **Check Audio Levels**: Ensure the audio levels are set correctly in the menu and that the internal microphone is enabled.

2. **Inspect External Microphone**: If using an external microphone, check the connection and battery (if applicable). Try a different microphone to determine if the issue lies with the microphone itself.

8. Error Messages
Common Error Messages:

- **"Cannot Use the Memory Card"**: Indicates a problem with the memory card.
- **"Camera Error"**: A general error that may require restarting the camera or checking settings.

Troubleshooting Steps:

1. **Follow On-Screen Instructions**: If an error message appears, follow any instructions provided on the screen.

2. **Restart the Camera**: Turn off the camera, remove the battery, wait a minute, and then power it back on.

3. **Inspect Power Switch**: Ensure the power switch is in the "On" position. If the camera still won't turn on, try a different battery if available.

2. Camera Freezes or Becomes Unresponsive
Possible Causes:

- Software glitch or firmware issue.

Troubleshooting Steps:

1. **Reset the Camera**: Turn the camera off, remove the battery, wait for about a minute, then reinsert the battery and power it back on.
2. **Update Firmware**: Check for any available firmware updates and install them, as they may resolve bugs causing the freeze.

3. Images are Blurry or Out of Focus
Possible Causes:

- Incorrect focus settings or camera shake.

Troubleshooting Steps:

1. **Check Focus Mode**: Ensure you are using the appropriate focus mode (e.g., autofocus or manual focus) for your shooting scenario.
2. **Stabilize the Camera**: If hand-holding the camera, consider using a tripod or stabilizer, especially in low-light conditions.
3. **Inspect Lens**: Clean the lens and check for any obstruction that may affect focus.

4. Memory Card Errors
Possible Causes:

- Corrupted memory card or incompatible card type.

Troubleshooting Steps:

1. **Format the Memory Card**: If you are experiencing issues, try formatting the memory card in the camera's settings (ensure to back up any important data first).
2. **Check Compatibility**: Ensure the memory card is compatible with the camera (e.g., SD, SDHC, or SDXC cards) and has a high enough speed class for your shooting mode (UHS-I or UHS-II recommended).

5. Battery Drains Quickly
Possible Causes:

- Power-hungry settings or features enabled.

Troubleshooting Steps:

4.2 Update the Camera Firmware

1. Insert the memory card with the firmware update back into the camera.
2. Turn on the camera.
3. Press the **Menu** button and navigate to the **Setup Menu**.
4. Select **Version** to check if the update file is recognized.
5. If the update is available, follow the on-screen prompts to start the installation process. Make sure not to turn off the camera or remove the memory card during the update.

4.3 Confirm Update Completion

- After the update process is complete, the camera will restart automatically. Check the firmware version again in the **Version** menu to confirm that the update was successful.

5. Post-Update Steps

After completing the firmware update:

- **Reset Settings (if needed)**: Sometimes, it's advisable to reset the camera settings to factory defaults to ensure compatibility with new features.
- **Test Functionality**: Check various functions and features of your camera to ensure everything is working smoothly.

Keeping the firmware of your **Sony Alpha A7CR/A7C II** updated is vital for maintaining the camera's performance and accessing new features. By following the outlined steps for checking and installing firmware updates, you can ensure that your camera operates optimally and remains at the forefront of technological advancements in photography and videography. Regular updates contribute to a seamless shooting experience and enhance your creative possibilities.

Troubleshooting Common Issues

While the Sony Alpha A7CR/A7C II is designed for high performance and reliability, users may occasionally encounter common issues. This section provides troubleshooting steps for some of the most frequent problems.

1. Camera Won't Turn On

Possible Causes:

- Dead battery or battery not installed properly.
- Faulty power switch.

Troubleshooting Steps:

1. **Check Battery**: Ensure the battery is fully charged. If not, charge it and try again.
2. **Reinstall Battery**: Remove the battery and reinsert it, ensuring it is seated correctly.

- New features that may enhance your photography or videography capabilities.

2. Checking for Firmware Updates

Before installing updates, check if your camera needs them:

2.1 Find Your Current Firmware Version

1. Turn on your camera and press the **Menu** button.
2. Navigate to the **Setup Menu** (the toolbox icon).
3. Select **Version** (usually at the bottom of the setup options) to view your current firmware version.

2.2 Check for Available Updates

- Visit the **Sony Support Website** for your specific camera model.
- Check the firmware section to see if a newer version is available compared to your current version.

3. Preparing for the Update

Before proceeding with the installation, make sure to prepare adequately:

3.1 Requirements

- A fully charged camera battery or an AC power adapter to ensure the camera doesn't power off during the update.
- A compatible memory card (preferably formatted in the camera).

3.2 Downloading the Firmware

1. Go to the **Sony Support Website**.
2. Locate your camera model and navigate to the firmware download section.
3. Download the latest firmware update file to your computer.
4. Extract the downloaded file if it's in a compressed format.

4. Installing the Firmware Update

Follow these steps to install the firmware update:

4.1 Transfer the Update to the Memory Card

1. Format the memory card in the camera to ensure compatibility.
2. Connect the memory card to your computer using a card reader.
3. Copy the extracted firmware update file to the root directory of the memory card.

2.1 Adjust Screen Settings

- **Lower Brightness**: Reduce the brightness of the LCD screen and EVF in the settings menu to conserve battery power.
- **Screen Timeout**: Set the camera to automatically turn off the screen after a short period of inactivity (e.g., 1-2 minutes).

2.2 Optimize Shooting Modes

- **Use Manual or Aperture Priority Mode**: Using manual settings can help you manage exposure without relying on power-hungry automatic adjustments.
- **Turn Off Continuous Shooting**: Switch to single-shot mode if continuous shooting is not necessary, as it consumes more battery.

2.3 Disable Unused Features

- **Turn Off Wi-Fi and Bluetooth**: Disable these features when not in use, as they drain battery power even when the camera is idle.
- **Limit Video Recording**: Video modes consume significantly more battery than still photography. Use video sparingly during shoots.

2.4 Use Energy-Efficient Settings

- **Disable Image Review**: Turn off the image review feature to prevent the display from lighting up after each shot.
- **Optimize Focus Settings**: Use manual focus, when possible, to conserve battery, as autofocus systems can be power-intensive.

3. Monitor Battery Health

3.1 Regular Checks

- Regularly check the battery health and performance by observing how long it lasts during regular use. If you notice a significant decrease in performance, it may be time for a replacement.

3.2 Cycle Count Awareness

- Keep track of your battery cycle count (the number of times the battery is charged and discharged). Most lithium-ion batteries last for 300-500 cycles before significant capacity loss occurs.

Being aware of the battery indicator and implementing effective power-saving strategies can significantly enhance the shooting experience with your **Sony Alpha A7CR/A7C II**. By monitoring battery levels and optimizing settings, you can ensure that your camera remains powered for longer periods, allowing you to focus on capturing stunning images and videos without interruptions.

4. Tips for Optimal Use
4.1 Monitor Power Levels

- Keep track of battery levels, both for the internal battery and the external power source, to ensure you don't run out of power unexpectedly.

4.2 Use Quality Accessories

- Invest in high-quality USB cables and power adapters to avoid compatibility issues and ensure reliable power delivery.

4.3 Avoid Overheating

- Be mindful of overheating, particularly when using the camera for extended periods while charging. Allow breaks between long sessions to keep the camera cool.

Utilizing external battery packs and USB charging with the **Sony Alpha A7CR/A7C II** can greatly enhance your shooting capabilities, offering extended power solutions for both photography and videography. By understanding how to effectively connect and use these options, you can ensure that your camera remains operational during critical moments, allowing you to capture every shot without interruption.

Battery Indicator and Power Saving Tips

The Sony Alpha A7CR/A7C II comes equipped with a battery indicator that provides crucial information about battery life, helping you manage your shooting sessions effectively. Here's how to understand the battery indicator and implement power-saving tips to maximize battery performance.

1. Understanding the Battery Indicator

The battery indicator on the **Sony Alpha A7CR/A7C II** helps you monitor the remaining battery life. Here's what you need to know:

1.1 Battery Level Display

- The battery level is displayed in the camera's menu and on the LCD screen, typically represented by a battery icon with several bars indicating the remaining charge:
    - **Full Charge**: All bars are filled.
    - **Medium Charge**: Some bars are empty.
    - **Low Charge**: One bar or no bars indicate a low battery.

1.2 Notifications

- The camera will provide a warning when the battery is running low, allowing you to take action (such as changing the battery or charging it) before it fully depletes.

2. Power Saving Tips

To extend battery life and make the most of your shooting time, consider the following power-saving tips:

1.1 USB Charging Options

- **USB Power Adapter**: Use a Sony-approved USB power adapter for optimal charging speed. Look for adapters with a minimum output of 5V/1.5A for efficient charging.

- **Power Banks**: High-capacity USB power banks can also charge the camera while in use. Choose a power bank with a minimum output of 5V/2A for faster charging capabilities.

1.2 Charging Process

- Connect the camera to the USB power source using a compatible USB-C cable.
- The camera can be used while charging, making it ideal for extended shoots.
- Ensure the camera is powered off during charging for optimal battery replenishment.

2. Using External Battery Packs

External battery packs can be used to power the camera directly, extending shooting time significantly.

2.1 Battery Packs Compatibility

- Choose external battery packs specifically designed for the **Sony Alpha A7CR/A7C II**, or those that support the NP-FZ100 battery. Some battery packs allow you to swap batteries while in use.

2.2 Connecting External Battery Packs

- **Powering the Camera**: Connect the external battery pack to the camera's USB-C port using a high-quality USB cable. Ensure that the power pack has sufficient output (5V/2A or higher).

- **Mounting Options**: Some battery packs come with mounting options that can attach to your tripod or camera rig, providing a stable setup while in use.

3. Benefits of External Power Solutions

3.1 Extended Shooting Time

- Using external battery packs allows for nearly unlimited shooting time, particularly useful for long events, travel, or time-lapse photography.

3.2 Reduced Battery Cycle Count

- Relying on external power sources reduces the frequency of charge cycles for your internal batteries, prolonging their overall lifespan.

3.3 Convenient Charging Options

- With USB charging capabilities, you can recharge the battery on-the-go, ensuring that you're always prepared for your next shot.

4. External Power Options
4.1 Battery Grips

- Consider using a battery grip compatible with the A7CR/A7C II, which can hold additional batteries and extend shooting time significantly.

4.2 USB Power Supply

- Use a USB power bank or an AC adapter for extended shoots or during studio sessions. This allows you to keep shooting without worrying about battery depletion.

5. Care and Maintenance
5.1 Proper Charging

- Use the official Sony charger or high-quality third-party chargers designed for the NP-FZ100 battery. Avoid overcharging and let the battery fully discharge occasionally to maintain optimal performance.

5.2 Store Batteries Properly

- If you're not using the battery for an extended period, store it in a cool, dry place and charge it to around 50% before storage to prevent degradation.

6. Monitor Battery Health
6.1 Battery Cycle Count

- Keep track of the number of charge cycles. Most lithium-ion batteries have a lifespan of around 300-500 charge cycles. If you notice a significant drop in battery life, it may be time for a replacement.

6.2 Use Battery Info Display

- Utilize the camera's battery info displays to monitor remaining battery percentage and usage statistics, allowing for better planning during shoots.

Maximizing battery performance for the Sony Alpha A7CR/A7C II requires a combination of settings adjustments, feature optimizations, and proper care practices. By implementing these strategies, you can extend your shooting time and ensure your camera is ready when inspiration strikes, allowing you to focus on capturing those perfect moments without worrying about battery life.

Using External Battery Packs and USB Charging

To enhance the shooting experience with the Sony Alpha A7CR/A7C II, utilizing external battery packs and USB charging can be highly beneficial. These options allow for extended shooting sessions, especially during events, travel, or prolonged filming. Here's how to effectively use these features:

1. Understanding USB Charging

The **Sony Alpha A7CR/A7C II** supports USB charging, allowing you to recharge the battery using a compatible USB power source.

CHAPTER TEN
BATTERY LIFE AND POWER MANAGEMENT

Maximizing Battery Performance

The Sony Alpha A7CR/A7C II is designed for high-performance photography and videography, but maximizing battery life is crucial for long shooting sessions. Here are some tips and techniques to extend the battery performance of your camera:

1. Understand Your Battery
1.1 Battery Specifications

- The **Sony Alpha A7CR/A7C II** typically uses the **NP-FZ100** battery, known for its high capacity and performance.

- Familiarize yourself with the estimated number of shots or video recording time you can achieve on a full charge (approximately 600 shots in normal shooting conditions).

2. Adjust Camera Settings
2.1 Screen and Viewfinder Settings

- **Lower Brightness**: Reduce the brightness of the LCD screen and electronic viewfinder (EVF) in the settings menu.

- **Auto Power Off**: Set the camera to automatically turn off after a short period of inactivity (e.g., 1 or 2 minutes).

2.2 Shooting Modes

- **Use Silent Shooting Mode**: This mode can reduce battery consumption during continuous shooting.

- **Choose Appropriate Shooting Modes**: If you're not in need of high frame rates, consider using Single Shot mode instead of Continuous Shooting.

3. Optimize Usage of Features
3.1 Wi-Fi and Bluetooth

- **Turn Off Wi-Fi/Bluetooth**: Disable these features when not in use, as they consume battery power even when the camera is idle.

3.2 Image Review

- **Limit Image Playback Time**: Reduce the duration for which images are displayed after taking a shot or disable image review altogether.

3.3 Lens Stabilization

- **Disable Optical SteadyShot (OSS)**: If you're using a tripod or stable surface, turn off lens stabilization to save battery.

...eries and Memory Cards

- **Batteries**: Always carry extra batteries for extended shooting sessions, especially during events or travel.

- **Memory Cards**: Use high-capacity and fast memory cards to handle 4K video and high-resolution images (e.g., SanDisk Extreme Pro or Lexar Professional).

Equipping your Sony Alpha A7CR/A7C II with quality tripods, gimbals, and other accessories can significantly enhance your photography and videography experience. By selecting the right gear tailored to your shooting style, you can achieve greater stability, creativity, and control, ultimately improving the quality of your images and videos. Whether you're a beginner or a seasoned professional, these accessories will help you get the most out of your camera.

- **Compatibility**: Ensure the gimbal is compatible with your camera and accessories.

3. Other Essential Accessories

Beyond tripods and gimbals, several other accessories can enhance your shooting experience with the **Sony Alpha A7CR/A7C II**.

3.1 Lens Filters

- **Polarizing Filters**: Reduce reflections and enhance colours, especially useful for landscape photography.
- **ND Filters**: Allow for longer exposures in bright conditions without overexposing the image.

3.2 External Microphones

- **Rode VideoMic Pro+**
    - **Type**: Directional On-Camera Microphone
    - **Features**:
        - High-quality audio capture for video recordings.
        - Built-in battery and easy mounting options.
- **Zoom H1n Handy Recorder**
    - **Type**: Portable Audio Recorder
    - **Features**:
        - Captures high-quality audio separately, perfect for interviews and vlogs.
        - Easy to use with a simple interface.

3.3 Camera Bags

- **Peak Design Everyday Backpack**
    - **Type**: Camera Backpack
    - **Features**:
        - Versatile and durable design with customizable compartments.
        - Comfortable to carry for long periods.
- **Lowepro ProTactic BP 450 AW II**
    - **Type**: All-Weather Backpack
    - **Features**:
        - Protective and spacious design with easy access.
        - Ideal for carrying multiple lenses and accessories.

- **Height Adjustability**: Look for tripods with adjustable height to suit various shooting situations.
- **Leg Locks**: Choose between twist locks or lever locks for ease of setup and adjustment.
- **Head Type**: Consider ball heads for flexibility or pan-tilt heads for precise control.

2. Gimbals

Gimbals are essential for achieving smooth, stabilized footage during video recording, particularly when moving or walking.

2.1 Recommended Gimbals

- **DJI Ronin-S**
    - **Type**: 3-Axis Gimbal
    - **Features**:
        - Supports a wide range of camera setups.
        - Smooth tracking and stabilization for dynamic shots.
        - Intuitive controls and customizable settings.
- **Zhiyun Crane 2S**
    - **Type**: 3-Axis Gimbal
    - **Features**:
        - High payload capacity for heavier camera setups.
        - Easy-to-use controls and touchscreen interface.
        - Versatile shooting modes, including vortex and time-lapse.
- **Moza AirCross 2**
    - **Type**: Lightweight 3-Axis Gimbal
    - **Features**:
        - Lightweight and portable design.
        - Multiple shooting modes for creative flexibility.
        - Long battery life for extended shooting sessions.

2.2 Features to Consider

- **Payload Capacity**: Ensure the gimbal can handle your camera and lens weight.
- **Battery Life**: Look for gimbals with longer battery life for extended use.
- **Ease of Setup**: Choose a gimbal that is easy to balance and operate.

professional-quality results in any shooting environment. By understanding your lighting options and techniques, you can significantly improve your creative capabilities and photographic outcomes.

Tripods, Gimbals, and Other Accessories

To maximize the capabilities of your Sony Alpha A7CR/A7C II, it's essential to equip yourself with the right accessories. Tripods, gimbals, and various other accessories can enhance stability, control, and creativity in your photography and videography. This guide covers recommended tripods, gimbals, and additional accessories that can help you get the most out of your camera.

1. Tripods

A sturdy tripod is essential for stable shooting, particularly in low-light conditions or when using long exposures.

1.1 Recommended Tripods

- **Manfrotto Befree Advanced**
  - **Type**: Travel Tripod
  - **Features**:
    - Compact and lightweight design, ideal for travel.
    - Quick setup and easy to carry.
    - Sturdy construction with adjustable leg angles.

- **Gitzo Traveler Series 1**
  - **Type**: Premium Travel Tripod
  - **Features**:
    - Made from high-quality carbon fibre for lightweight strength.
    - Compact design with excellent stability.
    - Suitable for heavier camera setups.

- **Benro Adventure Series**
  - **Type**: Versatile Tripod
  - **Features**:
    - Aluminium construction for durability.
    - Versatile leg angles for different terrains.
    - Easy to set up and adjust.

1.2 Features to Consider

- **Weight Capacity**: Ensure the tripod can support your camera and lens setup.

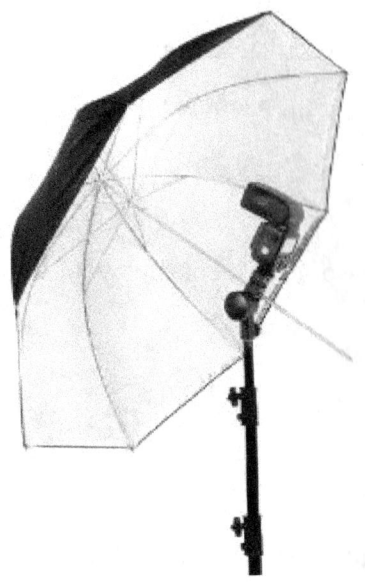

2.2 Light Stands and Mounts

- **Light Stands**
    - **Description**: Essential for positioning flash units and modifiers.
    - **Recommended Products**: Neewer Adjustable Light Stand, Manfrotto Light Stand.
- **Tripods for Flash**
    - **Description**: For stable mounting of off-camera flashes.
    - **Recommended Products**: Impact Heavy-Duty Tripod, Neewer 2-in-1 Tripod.

3. Tips for Using Flash and External Lighting

- **Understand Flash Modes**: Familiarize yourself with TTL and manual modes to control exposure effectively. TTL can save time during fast-paced shoots, while manual settings provide more control.
- **Use High-Speed Sync (HSS)**: For outdoor shooting in bright conditions, en_ HSS to use faster shutter speeds while still utilizing flash.
- **Bounce the Flash**: Instead of pointing the flash directly at your subje_ _nce the light off ceilings or walls to create softer, more natural lighting.
- **Experiment with Angles**: Move your light source around to se_ _it affects shadows and highlights. Different angles can dramatically change the mood_ photos.
- **Consider Lighting Ratios**: Use multiple lights to create _ _d dimension. Adjusting the power of each light source can help achieve desired co_ernal lighting solutions, enabling

The Sony Alpha A7CR/A7C II supports a variety of flash u_ _ opt for Sony's own flash units or you to enhance your photography in numerous ways. W_ _accessories will help you achieve third-party options, combining them with effectiv_

- Lightweight and battery-powered for location shoots.
- Excellent colour consistency and output quality.
- Wireless control with Profoto Air system.

2. Lighting Accessories

In addition to flash units, several accessories can enhance your lighting setup for various photography scenarios.

2.1 Light Modifiers

- **Softboxes**
    - **Description**: Diffuse the light for softer shadows and more flattering portraits.
    - **Recommended Products**: Godox 60x60cm Softbox, Neewer 32-inch Softbox.

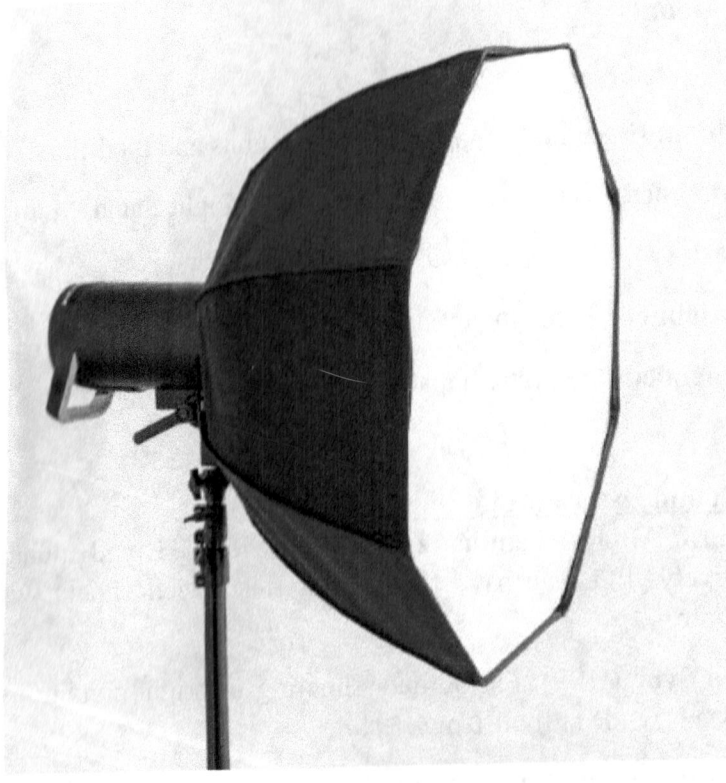

- **Umbrellas**
    - **Description**: Easy-to-use modifiers that can soften and spread light.
    - **Recommended Products**: Neewer 43-inch Umbrella, Godox Umbrella Softbox.
- **Diffusers**
    - **Description**: Attach to the flash to soften the light output.
    - **Recommended Products**: Gary Fong Lightsphere, MagMod MagSphere.

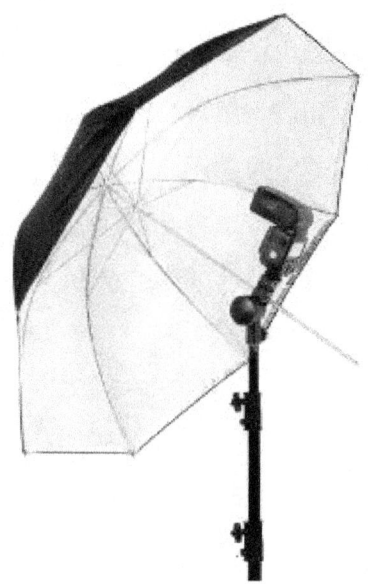

2.2 Light Stands and Mounts

- **Light Stands**
  - **Description**: Essential for positioning flash units and modifiers.
  - **Recommended Products**: Neewer Adjustable Light Stand, Manfrotto Light Stand.
- **Tripods for Flash**
  - **Description**: For stable mounting of off-camera flashes.
  - **Recommended Products**: Impact Heavy-Duty Tripod, Neewer 2-in-1 Tripod.

3. Tips for Using Flash and External Lighting

- **Understand Flash Modes**: Familiarize yourself with TTL and manual modes to control exposure effectively. TTL can save time during fast-paced shoots, while manual settings provide more control.

- **Use High-Speed Sync (HSS)**: For outdoor shooting in bright conditions, enable HSS to use faster shutter speeds while still utilizing flash.

- **Bounce the Flash**: Instead of pointing the flash directly at your subject, bounce the light off ceilings or walls to create softer, more natural lighting.

- **Experiment with Angles**: Move your light source around to see how it affects shadows and highlights. Different angles can dramatically change the mood of your photos.

- **Consider Lighting Ratios**: Use multiple lights to create depth and dimension. Adjusting the power of each light source can help achieve desired contrast.

The Sony Alpha A7CR/A7C II supports a variety of flash units and external lighting solutions, enabling you to enhance your photography in numerous ways. Whether you opt for Sony's own flash units or third-party options, combining them with effective lighting accessories will help you achieve

- Lightweight and battery-powered for location shoots.
- Excellent colour consistency and output quality.
- Wireless control with Profoto Air system.

2. Lighting Accessories

In addition to flash units, several accessories can enhance your lighting setup for various photography scenarios.

2.1 Light Modifiers

- **Softboxes**
    - **Description**: Diffuse the light for softer shadows and more flattering portraits.
    - **Recommended Products**: Godox 60x60cm Softbox, Neewer 32-inch Softbox.

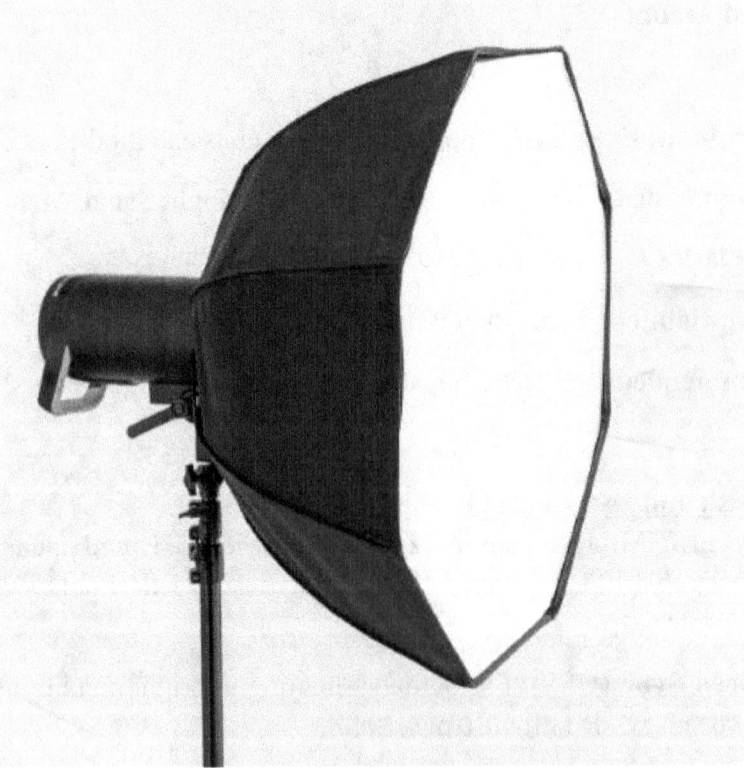

- **Umbrellas**
    - **Description**: Easy-to-use modifiers that can soften and spread light.
    - **Recommended Products**: Neewer 43-inch Umbrella, Godox Umbrella Softbox.
- **Diffusers**
    - **Description**: Attach to the flash to soften the light output.
    - **Recommended Products**: Gary Fong Lightsphere, MagMod MagSphere.

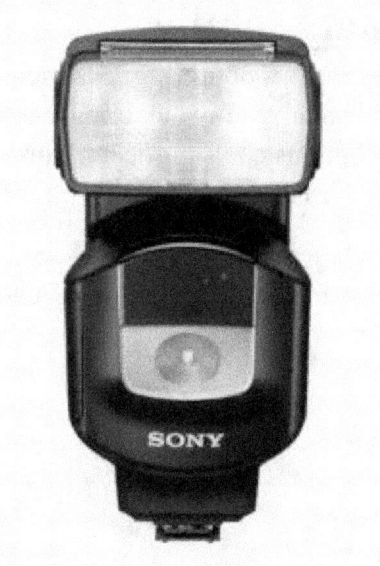

- **Sony HVL-F32M**
  - **Type**: On-Camera Flash
  - **Features**:
    - GN of 32, suitable for everyday photography.
    - Compact design, making it portable and easy to use.

1.2 Third-Party Flash Units

- **Godox V1-S**
  - **Type**: On-Camera Flash
  - **Features**:
    - Round head design for soft, even light distribution.
    - Built-in 2.4G wireless transmission for off-camera use.
    - TTL, HSS (High-Speed Sync), and manual modes.

- **Neewer NW-580**
  - **Type**: On-Camera Flash
  - **Features**:
    - Budget-friendly option with GN of 58.
    - TTL and manual modes for flexibility.
    - Supports remote triggering.

- **Profoto B10**
  - **Type**: Portable Studio Strobe
  - **Features**:

Flash Units and External Lighting

The Sony Alpha A7CR/A7C II offers various options for enhancing your photography with flash units and external lighting solutions. Whether you're shooting portraits, events, or low-light scenes, understanding the available lighting options can significantly improve your image quality. This guide covers compatible flash units, lighting accessories, and tips for effective lighting techniques.

1. Compatible Flash Units

Several flash units are compatible with the Sony Alpha A7CR/A7C II, ranging from on-camera speedlights to powerful studio strobes.

1.1 Sony Flash Units

- **Sony HVL-F60RM II**
    - **Type**: On-Camera Flash
    - **Features**:
        - High Guide Number (GN) of 60 for powerful illumination.
        - TTL (Through The Lens) metering for automatic exposure control.
        - Wireless radio control for off-camera flash setups.

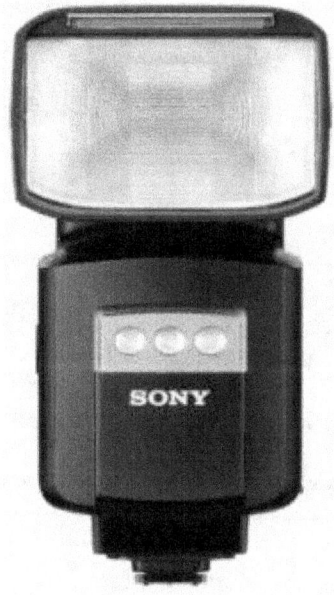

- **Sony HVL-F43RM**
    - **Type**: On-Camera Flash
    - **Features**:
        - GN of 43, compact and lightweight.
        - TTL and manual flash modes for versatile use.
        - Wireless control compatible with multiple flash units.

- **Sigma 24mm f/1.4 DG DN Art**: A high-quality wide-angle prime lens known for sharpness and bokeh.
            - **Sigma 35mm f/1.4 DG DN Art**: A popular standard prime lens with excellent low-light performance.
    - **Samyang/Rokinon**
        - **Examples**:
            - **Samyang 14mm f/2.8 AF**: An ultra-wide-angle autofocus lens, great for landscapes and astrophotography.
            - **Rokinon 85mm f/1.4 AF**: A fast portrait lens offering beautiful bokeh.
    - **Laowa**
        - **Examples**:
            - **Laowa 15mm f/4 Macro 1:1**: A unique macro lens that provides a wide angle and close-up capabilities.
            - **Laowa 24mm f/14 2x Macro**: A versatile macro lens for extreme close-ups.

3. Considerations When Using Adapters and Third-Party Lenses

When using lens adapters or third-party lenses, consider the following:

- **Compatibility**: Ensure the adapter is compatible with both your camera and the lens you wish to use.
- **Autofocus Performance**: Not all adapters support autofocus, and performance may vary. Check reviews for specific lens and adapter combinations.
- **Image Quality**: While many third-party lenses are excellent, some may not match the optical quality of native Sony lenses. Research and read reviews before purchasing.
- **Manual Focus**: Many adapted lenses may require manual focusing, which can be a different shooting experience.
- **Firmware Updates**: Some adapters may require firmware updates to maintain compatibility with the latest camera features.

The **Sony Alpha A7CR/A7C II** is highly versatile, allowing you to use a variety of lens adapters and third-party lenses to expand your creative options. Whether you're looking to adapt lenses from other systems or explore high-quality third-party options, there's a wide range of possibilities to enhance your photography experience. Always do your research to ensure compatibility and performance when selecting adapters and lenses for your setup.

- **Fotodiox Pro Lens Mount Adapter**
    - **Compatibility**: Adapts various lenses, including Canon, Nikon, and M42 screw mount lenses.
    - **Features**: Mechanical adapters; autofocus may not be available.

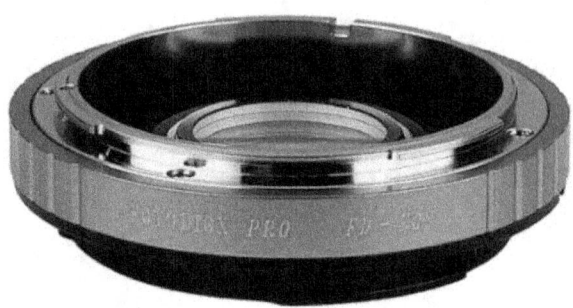

- **Sigma MC-11 Mount Converter**
    - **Compatibility**: Designed to use Canon EF-mount lenses on Sony E-mount bodies.
    - **Features**: Supports autofocus and image stabilization for compatible lenses.
- **Viltrox Lens Adapter**
    - **Compatibility**: Adapts Canon EF and Nikon F lenses to E-mount.
    - **Features**: Generally offers electronic communication for autofocus and aperture control.

2. Third-Party Lens Options for E-Mount

In addition to Sony's native E-mount lenses, several third-party manufacturers offer high-quality lenses specifically designed for E-mount systems:

2.1 Third-Party Lens Manufacturers

- **Tamron**
    - **Examples**:
        - **Tamron 28-75mm f/2.8 Di III RXD**: A versatile standard zoom lens with a fast aperture.
        - **Tamron 11-20mm f/2.8 Di III-A RXD**: An ultra-wide zoom lens ideal for landscapes and vlogging.
- **Sigma**
    - **Examples**:

- **Ideal For**: Landscape, architecture, and vlogging.

3. Lens Considerations
When selecting lenses for the **Sony Alpha A7CR/A7C II**, consider the following:

- **Focal Length**: Choose lenses based on your primary photography style (e.g., portraits, landscapes, macro).

- **Aperture**: A wider aperture (like f/1.8 or f/2.8) is beneficial for low-light conditions and achieving a shallow depth of field.

- **Weight and Size**: Consider the weight and size of the lens for portability, especially if you plan to shoot for extended periods.

- **Stabilization**: Some lenses come with Optical Steady Shot (OSS) for better stabilization, which is helpful for handheld shooting.

The Sony Alpha A7CR/A7C II is compatible with a wide range of E-mount lenses, offering photographers the flexibility to choose lenses that suit their creative needs. Whether you prefer prime, zoom, macro, or specialty lenses, there are numerous options available to help you achieve your photographic vision. Always consider your shooting style and preferences when selecting lenses to ensure you get the most out of your camera system.

Lens Adapters and Third-Party Options

The Sony Alpha A7CR/A7C II is compatible with various lens adapters that allow you to use lenses from different manufacturers. Additionally, many third-party manufacturers produce high-quality lenses designed specifically for the E-mount system. This guide provides an overview of lens adapters, third-party lens options, and considerations when using them.

1. Lens Adapters for E-Mount
Lens adapters enable the use of lenses from other systems on the Sony E-mount cameras. Here are some popular adapters:

1.1 Popular Lens Adapters

- **Metabones Smart Adapter**

    - **Compatibility**: Allows the use of Canon EF lenses on Sony E-mount cameras.

    - **Features**: Supports autofocus, image stabilization, and aperture control.

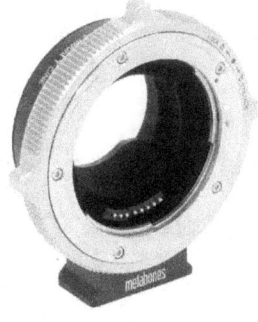

1.3 Macro Lenses

Macro lenses are designed for extreme close-ups, perfect for capturing fine details.

- **Sony FE 90mm f/2.8 Macro G OSS**
    - **Type**: Macro Lens
    - **Ideal For**: Close-up photography of flowers, insects, and small objects.

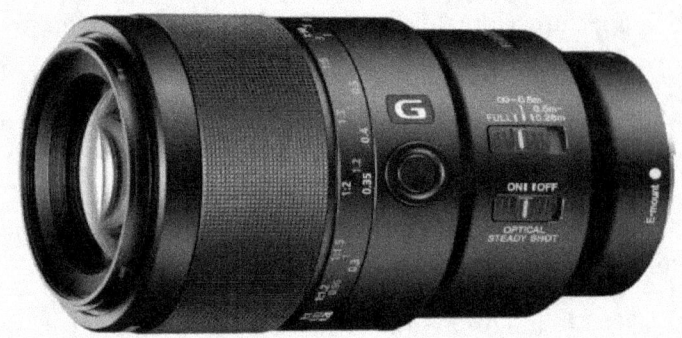

1.4 Specialty Lenses

These lenses cater to specific photography needs, such as tilt-shift or fisheye.

- **Sony E 10-18mm f/4 OSS**
    - **Type**: Ultra-Wide Zoom
    - **Ideal For**: Vlogging, landscape, and architecture photography.
- **Laowa 15mm f/4 Macro 1:1**
    - **Type**: Macro Lens
    - **Ideal For**: Wide-angle close-ups with a unique perspective.

2. Third-Party E-Mount Lenses

In addition to Sony's native lenses, several third-party manufacturers offer high-quality E-mount lenses.

- **Tamron 28-75mm f/2.8 Di III RXD**
    - **Type**: Standard Zoom
    - **Ideal For**: Versatile everyday shooting.
- **Sigma 24mm f/1.4 DG DN Art**
    - **Type**: Wide-Angle Prime
    - **Ideal For**: Landscape, astrophotography, and street photography.
- **Tamron 11-20mm f/2.8 Di III-A RXD**
    - **Type**: Ultra-Wide Zoom

- **Sony FE 85mm f/1.8**
    - **Type**: Telephoto Prime
    - **Ideal For**: Portraits with beautiful background blur (bokeh).

1.2 Zoom Lenses

Zoom lenses offer a range of focal lengths, making them versatile for various shooting situations.

- **Sony FE 24-70mm f/2.8 GM II**
    - **Type**: Standard Zoom
    - **Ideal For**: General-purpose photography, portraits, and events.

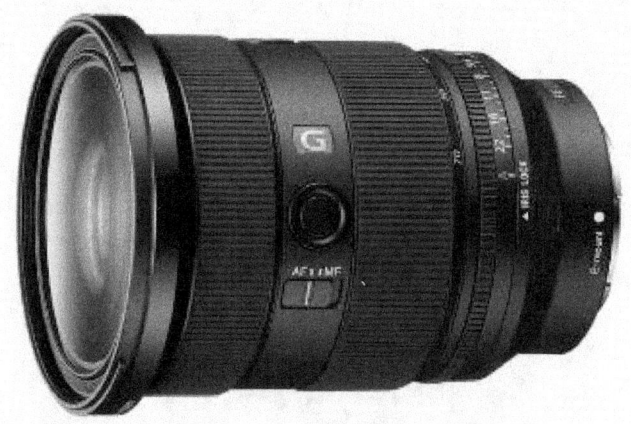

- **Sony FE 70-200mm f/2.8 GM OSS II**
    - **Type**: Telephoto Zoom
    - **Ideal For**: Sports, wildlife, and portrait photography.

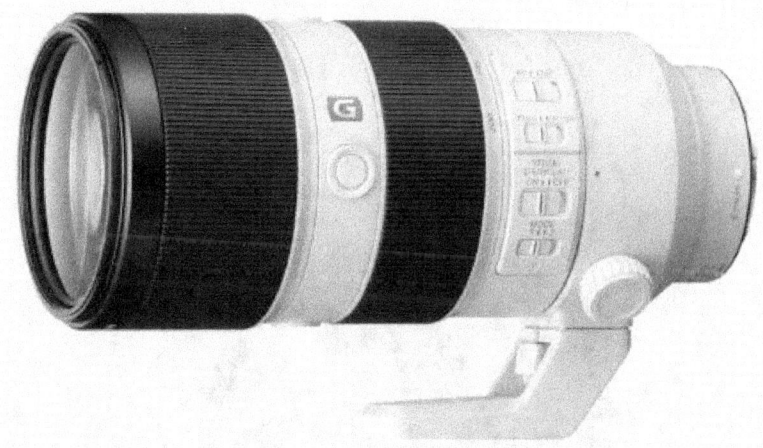

- **Sony 16-35mm f/2.8 GM**
    - **Type**: Wide-Angle Zoom
    - **Ideal For**: Landscape, architecture, and vlogging.

CHAPTER NINE
LENS AND ACCESSORIES

Compatible E-Mount Lenses

The Sony Alpha A7CR/A7C II uses the E-mount system, which is compatible with a wide range of lenses designed for both full-frame and APS-C sensor cameras. Here's an overview of the various categories of compatible E-mount lenses, along with some recommended options in each category.

1. Types of E-Mount Lenses
1.1 Prime Lenses

Prime lenses have a fixed focal length and are known for their sharpness and wider maximum apertures.

- **Sony FE 50mm f/1.8**
    - **Type**: Standard Prime
    - **Ideal For**: Portraits, street photography, and low-light conditions.

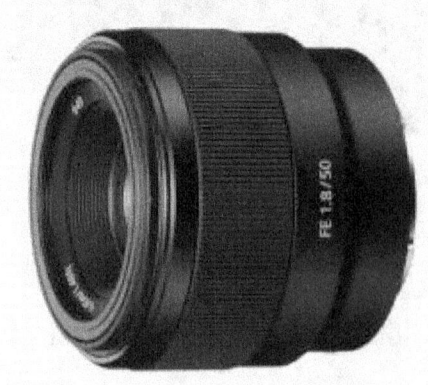

- **Sony FE 35mm f/1.8**
    - **Type**: Wide-Angle Prime
    - **Ideal For**: Landscape, architecture, and environmental portraits.

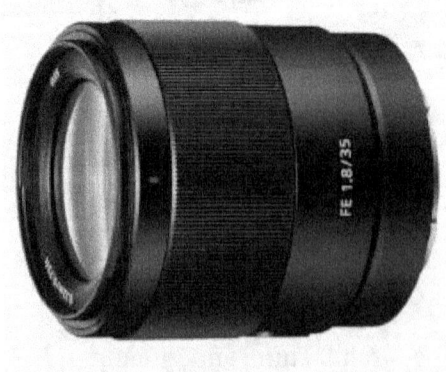

- **Learn Keyboard Shortcuts**: Familiarize yourself with shortcuts in Imaging Edge Desktop for quicker navigation and editing.
- **Experiment**: Don't be afraid to experiment with different editing techniques and styles to find what works best for you.
- **Backup Your Work**: Always back up original and edited files to prevent data loss.

Post-processing is a crucial step in maximizing the potential of your images captured with the Sony Alpha A7CR/A7C II. Utilizing Sony's imaging software, such as Imaging Edge Desktop and PlayMemories Home, allows for efficient editing, management, and enhancement of your photos and videos. By following the outlined workflows and tips, you can effectively refine your images and achieve your creative vision.

3. **Edit Colours**: Fine-tune the colour balance, saturation, and temperature to achieve the desired look.
4. **Apply Noise Reduction**: Reduce noise in high ISO images using the noise reduction tools.

Step 3: Advanced Editing

1. **Use Layers**: Create layers for non-destructive editing, allowing you to apply changes without affecting the original image.
2. **Crop and Straighten**: Crop the image for better composition and straighten any tilted horizons.
3. **Add Effects**: Apply creative effects, such as vignetting or graduated filters, to enhance the overall look.

Step 4: Exporting Images

1. **Save Changes**: Once you're satisfied with the edits, save the changes.
2. **Export Options**: Choose the export settings, including file format (e.g., JPEG, TIFF) and quality, before saving the final image.

3. Post-Processing Workflow with PlayMemories Home

For users of **PlayMemories Home**, the workflow is simpler and more focused on basic edits:

Step 1: Importing and Organizing

1. **Launch PlayMemories Home**: Open the software and select the import option.
2. **Organize Media**: Sort images and videos into albums or collections for easy access.

Step 2: Basic Editing

1. **Select an Image**: Click on the image you want to edit.
2. **Use Editing Tools**: Access tools for cropping, rotating, and adjusting brightness and contrast.
3. **Apply Simple Effects**: Add effects or filters as desired, keeping edits straightforward.

Step 3: Exporting and Sharing

1. **Save Changes**: Save your edited images.
2. **Share Options**: Utilize built-in sharing options to post images directly to social media or create slideshows for sharing

4. Tips for Effective Post-Processing

- **Stay Organized**: Maintain a structured folder system for your images to streamline the editing process.

1. **Sony Imaging Edge Desktop**
   - **Description**: A comprehensive software suite that allows users to edit and manage RAW images captured with Sony cameras.
   - **Key Features**:
     - **RAW Development**: Process RAW files with advanced editing options, including exposure, colour, and noise reduction adjustments.
     - **Image Management**: Organize and manage photo libraries, including tagging, rating, and filtering images.
     - **Batch Processing**: Apply settings to multiple images simultaneously, streamlining your workflow.
     - **Remote Shooting**: Control the camera remotely and capture images directly to your computer.

2. **Sony PlayMemories Home**
   - **Description**: A user-friendly software designed for managing and editing photos and videos.
   - **Key Features**:
     - **Easy Organization**: Sort images and videos by date, tags, and ratings.
     - **Basic Editing Tools**: Perform simple edits such as cropping, rotating, and colour adjustments.
     - **Slideshow Creation**: Compile images into slideshows with customizable transitions and effects.
     - **Social Sharing**: Easily share images on social media platforms

3. **Post-Processing Workflow with Imaging Edge Desktop**

To get started with post-processing using **Sony Imaging Edge Desktop**, follow these steps:

Step 1: Importing Images

1. **Launch the Software**: Open Imaging Edge Desktop on your computer.
2. **Import Images**: Use the import function to load your images from the camera or memory card. You can select individual files or entire folders.

Step 2: RAW Development

1. **Select an Image**: Click on a RAW file to open it in the editing workspace.
2. **Adjust Basic Settings**: Use sliders to adjust exposure, contrast, brightness, and other basic settings.

- **Function**: Add special effects such as miniature, fish-eye, or retro styles.
- **How to Use**: Access the picture effects menu, choose the effect you want, and apply it to the image.

7. Retouching Features

- **Function**: Use options like red-eye correction and blemish removal to enhance portraits.
- **How to Use**: Navigate to the retouching tools in the editing menu, select the specific feature, and follow on-screen instructions.

3. Saving Edited Images

After editing, you will typically have the option to:

- **Save as a New File**: Keep the original image intact by saving the edited version as a new file.
- **Overwrite the Original**: Replace the original image with the edited version if you're satisfied with the changes.

4. Tips for Effective In-Camera Editing

- **Keep It Simple**: While in-camera editing can be powerful, avoid over-editing. Aim for subtle adjustments that enhance your image without losing its original character.
- **Experiment**: Take the time to explore various editing options and see how they affect your images. This can lead to discovering unique styles and techniques.
- **Practice Non-Destructive Editing**: Always consider saving edited images as new files to retain the original for future adjustments.

The Sony Alpha A7CR/A7C II provides a range of in-camera image editing options that allow for quick adjustments and creative enhancements. By familiarizing yourself with these features, you can effectively improve your workflow, deliver polished images on the spot, and express your artistic vision without needing to rely solely on post-processing software. Embrace the in-camera editing capabilities to elevate your photography and achieve your desired results efficiently.

Post-Processing with Sony Imaging Software

Post-processing is an essential part of the photography workflow, especially when working with the Sony Alpha A7CR/A7C II. Sony provides several imaging software options that can help you edit, enhance, and manage your photos and videos efficiently. This guide will cover the main software options available for post-processing, their features, and tips for effective use.

Overview of Sony Imaging Software

Sony offers various software solutions to assist photographers and videographers in post-processing. The two primary applications are:

In-Camera Image Editing Options

The Sony Alpha A7CR/A7C II offers a variety of in-camera image editing options that allow photographers to enhance and customize their images without the need for external software. These features can be especially useful for quick adjustments, creative effects, or when you need to deliver images on the spot. This guide will explore the in-camera editing options available on your camera.

1. Accessing In-Camera Editing Options
To access the in-camera editing options:

1. **View an Image**: After capturing an image, press the **Playback button** to review your photos.
2. **Access the Editing Menu**: Press the **Menu button**, then navigate to the **Playback menu** where you'll find editing options.

2. Key In-Camera Editing Features
Here are some of the main editing options available on the A7CR/A7C II:

1. Cropping

- **Function**: Adjust the composition of your image by cropping unwanted areas.
- **How to Use**: Select the crop option in the editing menu, then use the joystick or touch screen to select the crop area.

2. Adjusting Brightness and Contrast

- **Function**: Fine-tune the exposure and contrast to enhance the image's overall look.
- **How to Use**: Access the brightness/contrast adjustment feature, then use sliders to increase or decrease levels as needed.

3. Colour Adjustments

- **Function**: Modify saturation, hue, and temperature to achieve desired colour effects.
- **How to Use**: Navigate to the colour adjustment settings, and use sliders to tweak saturation and temperature according to your preference.

4. Adding Creative Filters

- **Function**: Apply various creative filters and effects to enhance the artistic quality of your images.
- **How to Use**: Access the filter options, browse through available effects (such as sepia, black and white, vivid), and select the desired one to apply to your image.

5. Vignetting

- **Function**: Darken or lighten the edges of the image to draw attention to the centre.
- **How to Use**: Locate the vignetting adjustment option, and use sliders to increase or decrease the effect.

6. Picture Effects

- **Smaller File Size**: JPEG files are significantly smaller than RAW files, allowing you to store more images on your memory card and use less storage space on your computer.

- **Immediate Usability**: JPEG images are ready to use straight out of the camera, requiring little to no post-processing.

- **Faster Processing and Transfer**: JPEG files can be processed and transferred more quickly due to their smaller size, which is advantageous for fast-paced shooting situations (e.g., events or sports).

- **Universal Compatibility**: JPEG is a widely used format compatible with virtually all devices, software, and online platforms.

4. Considerations for Choosing Between RAW and JPEG

- **Purpose of Shooting**: If you're shooting for professional work or high-quality prints, RAW is usually the best option. For casual photography, social media, or situations where speed is essential, JPEG may suffice.

- **Post-Processing Workflow**: If you enjoy editing your photos and require extensive adjustments, RAW is the way to go. If you prefer minimal editing, JPEG can save you time.

- **Storage and Memory Card Speed**: If you're limited on storage space or using a slower memory card, JPEG allows for more images to be saved without compromising performance.

- **Shooting Conditions**: In challenging lighting situations, RAW can help recover highlights and shadows that may be lost in JPEG.

5. Best Practices for Shooting in RAW and JPEG

- **Set Up Dual-Format Shooting**: The A7CR/A7C II allows you to shoot in both RAW and JPEG simultaneously. This gives you the flexibility to have high-quality files for editing while also having ready-to-use images.

- **Manage Storage**: Be mindful of the space on your memory cards when shooting in RAW, as they take up significantly more space than JPEG files.

- **Use Efficient Workflow Software**: Consider using software like Adobe Lightroom or Capture One to manage and edit RAW files efficiently.

Choosing between RAW and JPEG on the Sony Alpha A7CR/A7C II ultimately depends on your specific photography needs, workflow preferences, and the intended use of your images.

By understanding the differences and benefits of each format, you can make informed decisions that enhance your photography experience and produce high-quality results. Whether you opt for the flexibility of RAW or the convenience of JPEG, both formats offer unique advantages to cater to different shooting scenarios.

The **Sony Alpha A7CR/A7C II** provides versatile Picture Profiles and Creative Styles that allow you to customize your images and videos significantly. By understanding how to access and apply these settings, you can enhance your creative output and better achieve your artistic vision. Explore the various options available, experiment with combinations, and take full advantage of the camera's capabilities to elevate your photography and videography projects.

RAW vs JPEG Shooting

When using the Sony Alpha A7CR/A7C II, photographers must decide between shooting in RAW or JPEG format. Each format has its advantages and disadvantages, and the choice can significantly impact your workflow and the final quality of your images. This guide will break down the differences between RAW and JPEG, helping you make an informed decision based on your needs.

1. Understanding RAW and JPEG Formats

RAW Format:

- **Definition**: RAW files are uncompressed and contain all the data captured by the camera's sensor at the time of exposure. They are often referred to as digital negatives.

- **File Extension**: Common extensions include. ARW (Sony RAW format) and others depending on the camera.

JPEG Format:

- **Definition**: JPEG files are compressed images that discard some data to reduce file size. They are processed in-camera, meaning that the image has undergone adjustments like contrast and saturation.

- **File Extension**: Common extension is .JPEG or .JPG.

2. Advantages of Shooting in RAW

- **Higher Image Quality**: RAW files maintain more detail and dynamic range, allowing for greater quality in post-processing.

- **Extensive Editing Flexibility**: Because RAW files contain unprocessed data, you have more latitude in adjusting exposure, white balance, contrast, and colour grading without losing quality.

- **Better for High Dynamic Range (HDR)**: The extra data in RAW files makes them ideal for HDR photography, where capturing a wider range of tones is essential.

- **Non-Destructive Editing**: Edits made to RAW files do not affect the original image data, allowing for reversible adjustments.

3. Advantages of Shooting in JPEG

2. Understanding Creative Styles

Creative Styles are preset configurations primarily aimed at still photography. They enhance the look of your images through adjustments in colour, contrast, brightness, and saturation.

Key Features of Creative Styles:

- **Standard**: The default setting for balanced images.
- **Vivid**: Increases saturation and contrast for vibrant collars.
- **Portrait**: Optimized for skin tones, providing a softer look.
- **Landscape**: Enhances blues and greens for a more dynamic landscape appearance.
- **Night Scene**: Optimizes settings for low-light shooting.
- **Black & White**: Captures monochrome images with contrast adjustments.

How to Access and Set Creative Styles:

1. **Access the Menu**:
   - Press the **Menu Button**.
2. **Navigate to Creative Style Settings**:
   - Go to **Camera Settings** > **Creative Style**.
3. **Select a Style**:
   - Choose a Creative Style from the list (Standard, Vivid, Portrait, etc.).
4. **Customize Settings** (if desired):
   - Adjust parameters like contrast, saturation, and sharpness for the selected style.
5. **Save Changes**:
   - Confirm your settings to apply them.

3. Tips for Using Picture Profiles and Creative Styles

- **Experiment with Different Settings**: Try various Picture Profiles and Creative Styles to find the one that best suits your shooting scenario and personal style.
- **Consider Post-Production Needs**: If you plan to colour grade your footage later, consider using S-Log profiles for greater dynamic range.
- **Utilize Custom Profiles**: Create and save custom profiles based on your specific shooting conditions to streamline your workflow.
- **Test Before Important Shoots**: Conduct test shots with different profiles to ensure you achieve the desired look before your main shoot.

CHAPTER EIGHT
IMAGE PROCESSING AND EDITING

Picture Profiles and Creative Styles

The Sony Alpha A7CR/A7C II offers a range of Picture Profiles and Creative Styles that enhance your imaging experience by allowing you to customize the appearance of your photos and videos. Understanding these settings can help you achieve your desired aesthetic and make your content stand out. This guide will cover the different Picture Profiles and Creative Styles, how to apply them, and tips for effective use.

1. Understanding Picture Profiles

Picture Profiles are preset configurations that adjust various camera settings, including gamma, colour, and detail, primarily for video recording. They allow filmmakers to achieve specific looks and optimize footage for post-production.

Key Features of Picture Profiles:

- **Gamma Settings**: Control the overall brightness and contrast of the footage. Common gamma options include S-Log2, S-Log3, and Cine gamma profiles, which offer greater dynamic range and flexibility in colour grading.

- **Colour Mode**: Adjusts colour settings to achieve different looks, such as standard, vivid, or muted colours.

- **Detail Level**: Sets the sharpness and clarity of the image, allowing for a softer or more defined appearance.

- **Skin Tone**: Optimizes colours specifically for capturing natural skin tones.

How to Access and Set Picture Profiles:

1. **Access the Menu**:
    - Press the **Menu Button**.

2. **Navigate to Picture Profile Settings**:
    - Go to **Camera Settings** > **Picture Profile**.

3. **Select a Profile**:
    - Choose a Picture Profile from the list (PP1 to PP10).

4. **Customize Settings**:
    - You can adjust gamma, colour mode, detail, and other parameters for the selected profile.

5. **Save Changes**:
    - Confirm your settings to apply them.

4. Configuring HDMI Output Settings

To ensure the best performance and compatibility, configure the HDMI output settings on your camera.

Step-by-Step Configuration

1. **Access the Menu**:
   - Press the **Menu Button** on the camera.

2. **Navigate to HDMI Settings**:
   - Go to **Setup** > **HDMI Settings**.

3. **Select HDMI Resolution**:
   - Choose the desired resolution (e.g., 4K, 1080p) based on your needs and the capabilities of your external monitor.

4. **Choose Output Options**:
   - Select options such as **Clean HDMI Output** to remove on-screen displays (like menus and settings) for a clearer image.
   - Ensure **4K Output** (if applicable) is enabled for maximum resolution.

5. **Adjust Frame Rate** (if applicable):
   - Depending on your recording needs, set the desired frame rate for video output.

5. Using External Monitors Effectively

When using an external monitor, consider the following tips for optimal performance:

- **Adjust Monitor Settings**: Set brightness, contrast, and color settings on the external monitor to suit your shooting environment.

- **Use Peaking and Zebra Functions**: Enable focus peaking and zebra patterns on your camera to assist with manual focus and exposure when monitoring through the external display.

- **Secure Cables**: Ensure that HDMI cables are securely connected to prevent accidental disconnection during use.

- **Test Your Setup**: Before important shoots, test the entire setup to ensure that the connection is stable and functioning as expected.

Connecting the Sony Alpha A7CR/A7C II to external monitors via HDMI provides enhanced monitoring and recording capabilities, making it ideal for professional shoots and presentations. By following the steps outlined in this guide, you can easily set up and configure your camera for optimal performance. Embrace the advantages of external monitoring to elevate your photography and videography experience.

Connecting to HDMI and External Monitors

The Sony Alpha A7CR/A7C II features HDMI output, allowing you to connect the camera to external monitors or recording devices for enhanced viewing and monitoring capabilities. This guide will help you understand how to connect your camera to HDMI devices, configure settings, and optimize your setup for various shooting scenarios.

1. Understanding HDMI Output Options

The A7CR/A7C II has a **Type-A HDMI output**, which allows for direct connection to compatible external monitors, recorders, and other devices.

Key Uses:

- **Live Monitoring**: View your camera's live feed on a larger screen during shoots.
- **Video Recording**: Capture high-quality video externally for professional projects.
- **Presentations**: Use an external monitor for displaying your photos and videos during presentations or workshops.

2. Required Equipment

To connect your camera to an HDMI device, you will need:

- **HDMI Cable**: A compatible Type-A HDMI cable.
- **External Monitor or Recorder**: Ensure the device you are connecting to has an HDMI input.

3. Connecting the Camera to an External Monitor

Step-by-Step Connection Process

1. **Power Off the Devices**: Turn off both the camera and the external monitor or recorder before making any connections.
2. **Connect the HDMI Cable**:
    - Plug one end of the **HDMI cable** into the **HDMI output port** on the camera.
    - Connect the other end of the cable to the **HDMI input port** on the external monitor or recorder.
3. **Power On the Devices**:
    - Turn on the external monitor or recorder first, then power on the camera.
4. **Select the HDMI Input**:
    - On the external monitor, select the HDMI input source that corresponds to the port where you connected the camera.

Using the Remote-Control Interface

1. **Access Remote Shooting**:
    - Select the **Remote Shooting** option in the app. The camera's live view will appear on your smartphone screen.

2. **Adjust Camera Settings**:
    - Use the app to adjust settings like focus, exposure, and shooting mode. Look for icons representing these settings on the app interface.

3. **Capture Photos**:
    - Press the shutter button displayed on your smartphone screen to take a photo. The camera will capture the image, and you can view it in the app afterward.

3. Advanced Features in Imaging Edge App

In addition to basic remote-control features, the Imaging Edge app provides advanced functionalities:

- **Focus Control**: Tap on the screen in the app to select a focus point directly.

- **Histogram and Level Gauge**: Display real-time histogram and level gauge on the app for better exposure and composition.

- **Adjusting Image Quality**: Change image quality settings, such as JPEG/RAW format, directly from the app.

- **Time-Lapse and Interval Shooting**: Set up time-lapse photography or interval shooting to capture sequences over time.

4. Tips for Effective Remote-Control Shooting

- **Stable Connection**: Ensure your smartphone remains within the Wi-Fi range of the camera for a stable connection.

- **Battery Management**: Monitor battery levels on both devices to avoid interruptions during shooting sessions.

- **Test Before Shooting**: Before important shoots, conduct a test to confirm that the remote-control features are functioning correctly.

- **Use a Tripod**: For optimal stability during remote shooting, consider using a tripod to avoid camera shake.

The **Imaging Edge App** greatly enhances the usability of the **Sony Alpha A7CR/A7C II** by allowing for remote control functionality. By following the setup process and exploring the app's features, you can take full advantage of this technology to create stunning images and videos with ease. Embrace the flexibility and convenience that remote shooting offers, enhancing your photography experience and creativity.

Using Imaging Edge App for Remote Control

The Imaging Edge App enhances your experience with the Sony Alpha A7CR/A7C II by providing remote control capabilities, allowing you to shoot photos and videos from your smartphone. This guide will walk you through setting up the app for remote control, its features, and tips for effective use.

1. Setting Up the Imaging Edge App

To get started with remote control using the Imaging Edge app, follow these steps:

Step-by-Step Setup

1. **Download the App**:
    - Download and install the **Imaging Edge Mobile** app from the **Google Play Store** (Android) or **Apple App Store** (iOS).

2. **Prepare the Camera**:
    - Ensure the **Sony Alpha A7CR/A7C II** is powered on.
    - Access the **Menu** > **Network Settings** > **Wi-Fi Settings** and turn on the Wi-Fi function.

3. **Select Connection Method**:
    - Choose **Smartphone Connection** from the Wi-Fi settings. The camera will display an SSID and password or a QR code for connection.

4. **Connect Your Smartphone**:
    - On your smartphone, go to **Wi-Fi settings**, find the camera's SSID, and enter the password to connect. Alternatively, scan the QR code if provided.

5. **Open the Imaging Edge App**:
    - Launch the app on your smartphone and follow any prompts to establish a connection with your camera.

2. Accessing Remote Control Features

Once your smartphone is connected to the camera through the Imaging Edge app, you can access various remote-control features.

Key Features

- **Live View Display**: The app will show a live view from your camera, allowing you to frame your shots accurately.

- **Camera Controls**: Adjust settings such as shutter speed, aperture, ISO, and focus mode directly from your smartphone.

- **Capture Images**: Take photos and videos using the app's shutter button.

- **Self-Timer Functionality**: Set a timer for capturing images, useful for group shots or selfies.

- In the Imaging Edge Mobile app, select the **Remote Shooting** option.
- The app will display the live view from your camera, allowing you to frame your shot.

3. **Adjust Camera Settings**:
    - You can adjust various camera settings directly through the app, including:
        - **Shutter Speed**
        - **Aperture**
        - **ISO**
        - **Focus Mode**
        - **Shooting Mode** (Single shot, Continuous, etc.)

4. **Capture Images**:
    - To take a photo, press the shutter button on your smartphone's screen.
    - The camera will capture the image, and you will see a preview in the app.

5. **Use Additional Features**:
    - Explore other features available in remote shooting, such as:
        - **Self-timer**: Set a delay for capturing images.
        - **Focus control**: Adjust focus points directly from the app.

3. Tips for Using Wireless File Transfer and Remote Shooting

- **Stay Within Range**: Ensure that your smartphone stays within the Wi-Fi range of the camera for a stable connection.

- **Monitor Battery Levels**: Both the camera and smartphone can consume battery quickly during file transfers and remote shooting. Keep an eye on battery levels and have a backup if needed.

- **Test the Setup**: Before important shoots, test the wireless connection and app functionality to ensure everything works smoothly.

- **Use Airplane Mode**: When not using Wi-Fi or Bluetooth, consider putting your smartphone in airplane mode to conserve battery life.

The **Sony Alpha A7CR/A7C II** provides a seamless experience for wireless file transfer and remote shooting using your smartphone. By following the steps outlined above, you can enhance your shooting capabilities and streamline your workflow. Embrace these features to enjoy the flexibility of remote control and the convenience of easy file sharing, allowing you to focus more on your creativity and less on the logistics.

1. Setting Up Wireless File Transfer

Wireless file transfer enables you to send photos and videos from your camera to your smartphone quickly.

Step-by-Step Guide

1. **Download the Imaging Edge Mobile App**:
   - Ensure you have the **Imaging Edge Mobile** app installed on your smartphone. Available on both **iOS** and **Android** platforms.

2. **Connect the Camera to Your Smartphone**:
   - **Turn on the Camera**: Ensure your camera is powered on.
   - **Enable Wi-Fi**: Access the **Menu** > **Network Settings** > **Wi-Fi Settings** and turn on the Wi-Fi function.
   - **Select Connection Method**: Choose **Smartphone Connection**. The camera will display an SSID and password or a QR code.
   - **Connect Your Smartphone**: On your smartphone, go to **Wi-Fi settings**, find the camera's SSID, and enter the password to connect. Alternatively, scan the QR code if available.

3. **Open Imaging Edge Mobile**:
   - Launch the Imaging Edge Mobile app on your smartphone.
   - Follow the prompts to establish a connection with your camera. The app should detect the camera automatically.

4. **Transfer Files**:
   - In the app, select **Send to Smartphone**.
   - Choose the images or videos you want to transfer. You can select multiple files or all at once.
   - Confirm the transfer. The selected files will be sent to your smartphone's gallery.

2. Remote Shooting with Smartphone

Remote shooting allows you to control your camera and capture images directly from your smartphone, providing greater flexibility and creative options.

Step-by-Step Guide

1. **Ensure Connectivity**:
   - Confirm that your smartphone is connected to the camera via Wi-Fi and that the Imaging Edge Mobile app is open.

2. **Access Remote Shooting**:

4. **Enable Bluetooth**:
    - Turn on the **Bluetooth Function**.

5. **Pair with a Device**:
    - Select **Pairing** and follow the prompts to start pairing with your smartphone or tablet.
    - On your smartphone, ensure Bluetooth is turned on, then look for the camera in the available devices list and pair them.

3. Remote Control and File Transfer

Once your camera is connected via Wi-Fi or Bluetooth, you can use various features for remote control and file transfer.

Remote Shooting:

- Use the Imaging Edge Mobile app to control the camera remotely. You can adjust settings, capture photos, and start/stop video recording from your smartphone.

File Transfer:

- Quickly transfer images and videos from the camera to your smartphone for easy sharing on social media or cloud storage.

4. Tips for Using Wi-Fi and Bluetooth

- **Maintain Good Signal**: Ensure you are within range of the camera's Wi-Fi signal to maintain a stable connection.
- **Check Battery Levels**: Using Wi-Fi and Bluetooth can drain the camera's battery. Keep an eye on battery levels, especially during long shoots.
- **Update Firmware**: Regularly check for firmware updates for your camera and the Imaging Edge app to ensure compatibility and access to new features.
- **Use Airplane Mode**: To conserve battery life, consider using airplane mode when not transferring files or controlling the camera remotely.

The **Sony Alpha A7CR/A7C II** offers convenient Wi-Fi and Bluetooth connectivity features that enhance your photography and videography experience. By following the setup procedures for these functions, you can easily share your work, control your camera remotely, and streamline your workflow. Embracing these technologies will elevate your creative projects and allow for more efficient sharing and collaboration.

Wireless File Transfer and Remote Shooting with Smartphone

The Sony Alpha A7CR/A7C II allows you to wirelessly transfer files and control your camera remotely using your smartphone. This feature enhances your shooting flexibility and simplifies sharing your work. This guide will walk you through the steps for wireless file transfer and remote shooting using your smartphone.

- Choose **Smartphone Connection** or **PC Remote** based on your device. If you're connecting to a smartphone, select **Smartphone Connection**.

7. **Connect to a Device**:

   - The camera will generate a QR code or SSID and password that you can use to connect your smartphone or computer to the camera's Wi-Fi network.

   - On your smartphone, go to **Wi-Fi settings**, find the camera's SSID, and enter the password to connect.

Using the Imaging Edge Mobile App

To enable advanced features like remote shooting and easy file transfers, download the Imaging Edge Mobile app from your device's app store.

1. **Open the App**: Launch the Imaging Edge Mobile app on your smartphone.

2. **Follow the On-Screen Instructions**: Follow the prompts to connect the app to your camera.

3. **Grant Permissions**: Allow necessary permissions for photo access and notifications.

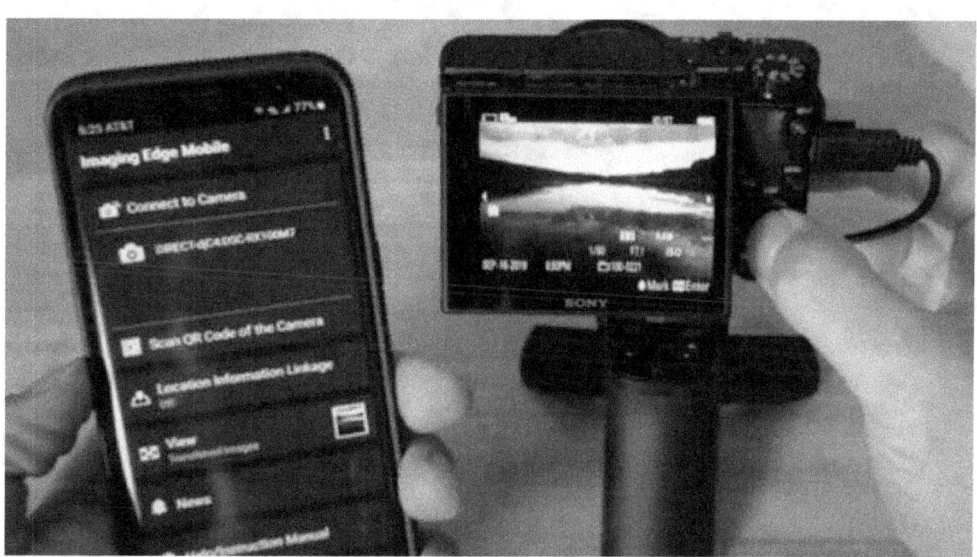

2. Setting Up Bluetooth Connectivity

Bluetooth connectivity allows for a stable connection with your smartphone, enabling remote control and easy transfer of images without the need for Wi-Fi.

Connecting via Bluetooth

1. **Access the Menu**: Press the **Menu Button** on the camera.

2. **Navigate to Network Settings**:

   - Go to **Network Settings**.

3. **Select Bluetooth Settings**:

   - Choose **Bluetooth Settings** from the options.

CHAPTER SEVEN
CONNECTIVITY FEATURES

Built-in Wi-Fi and Bluetooth Setup

The Sony Alpha A7CR/A7C II features built-in Wi-Fi and Bluetooth connectivity, allowing for seamless sharing of photos and videos, remote control of the camera, and easy file transfer to compatible devices. This guide will walk you through the setup process for both Wi-Fi and Bluetooth features, ensuring you can take full advantage of these functionalities.

1. Setting Up Wi-Fi Connectivity

The Wi-Fi feature on the A7CR/A7C II enables you to connect the camera to your smartphone, tablet, or computer for file transfer and remote shooting.

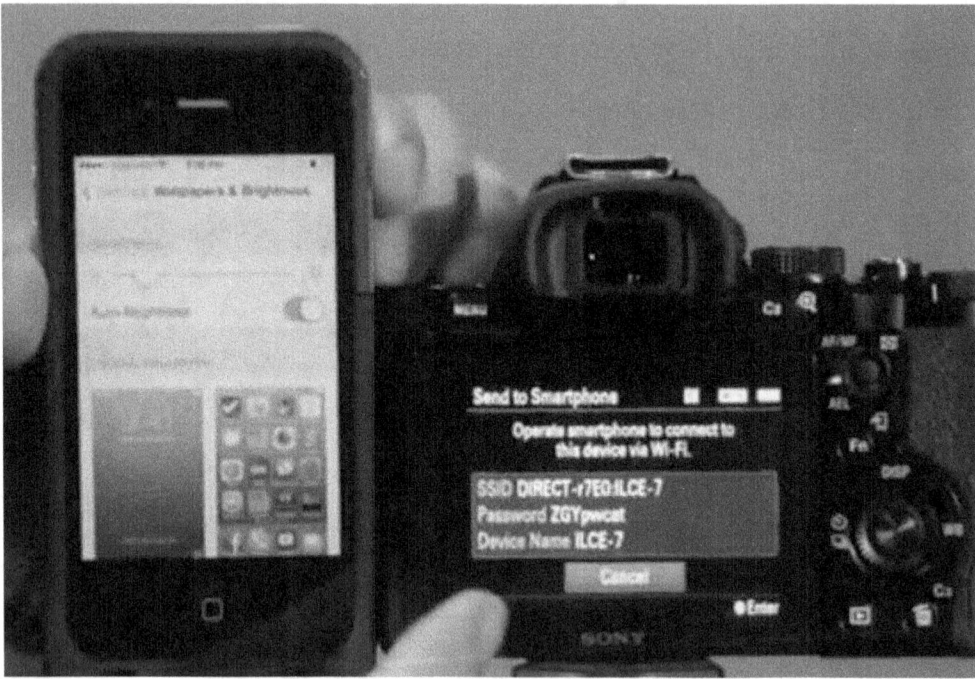

Connecting to Wi-Fi

1. **Turn on the Camera**: Ensure your camera is powered on.
2. **Access the Menu**: Press the **Menu Button**.
3. **Navigate to Network Settings**:
   - Go to **Network Settings** (the icon typically looks like a globe or a Wi-Fi signal).
4. **Select Wi-Fi Settings**:
   - Choose **Wi-Fi Settings** from the options.
5. **Enable Wi-Fi**:
   - Turn on the **Wi-Fi Function** to activate the Wi-Fi feature.
6. **Select Connection Method**:

CHAPTER TWELVE
CONCLUSION AND TIPS

Best Practices for Shooting with the A7CR/A7C II

To maximize the performance and capabilities of your Sony Alpha A7CR/A7C II, it's essential to adopt best practices that enhance your shooting experience. Here are some key tips for various aspects of photography and videography:

1. Familiarize Yourself with the Camera

- **Read the Manual**: Spend time understanding the features and functions of your camera through the user manual. Familiarity will help you utilize the camera effectively.

- **Customize Settings**: Tailor the camera settings to your shooting style. Customize function buttons for quick access to your most-used settings.

2. Use the Right Shooting Modes

- **Choose the Appropriate Mode**:
    - Use **Auto Mode** for easy shooting, **Program Mode** for some manual control, and **Manual Mode** for complete creative freedom.
    - Experiment with **Aperture Priority** and **Shutter Priority** modes to control depth of field and motion blur effectively.

3. Optimize Focus Settings

- **Utilize Eye AF**: Make use of the Eye Autofocus feature for portraits to ensure sharp focus on the subject's eyes.

- **Experiment with Focus Points**: Use flexible focus points for more control over your composition and focus areas, especially in complex scenes.

4. Master Exposure Settings

- **Understand Exposure Triangle**: Familiarize yourself with the relationship between aperture, shutter speed, and ISO. Balance these settings to achieve the desired exposure.

- **Use Exposure Compensation**: Adjust exposure compensation for scenes with high contrast to prevent highlights from blowing out or shadows from losing detail.

5. Utilize the Vari-Angle LCD Screen

- **Compose Unique Angles**: Take advantage of the vari-angle LCD screen to shoot from high or low angles easily.

- **Use Live View**: In challenging lighting conditions, use Live View to accurately preview exposure and focus.

6. Maintain Stability

- **Use a Tripod or Stabilizer**: For long exposures or video shooting, use a tripod or gimbal to minimize camera shake and ensure stability.
- **Utilize In-Body Stabilization**: The A7CR/A7C II features in-body image stabilization (IBIS). Activate it when shooting handheld to help reduce blur.

7. Optimize Your Settings for Low Light

- **Increase ISO**: Don't hesitate to increase ISO in low-light conditions. The A7CR/A7C II performs well at higher ISO settings.
- **Use Wider Apertures**: Open the aperture to allow more light to hit the sensor, which can help in dim environments.

8. Manage Battery Life

- **Use Power Saving Features**: Enable power-saving settings to extend battery life during shoots.
- **Carry Extra Batteries**: Always have spare batteries, especially for long shoots or when traveling.

9. Utilize Post-Processing

- **Shoot in RAW**: Capture images in RAW format for more flexibility in post-processing, allowing greater control over exposure and color adjustments.
- **Use Sony Imaging Software**: Take advantage of Sony's software for editing and organizing your photos to maximize image quality.

10. Regular Maintenance

- **Keep Gear Clean**: Regularly clean the lens and sensor to prevent dust spots from appearing in your images.
- **Update Firmware**: Stay informed about firmware updates to ensure your camera has the latest features and improvements.

By following these best practices for shooting with your **Sony Alpha A7CR/A7C II**, you can enhance your photography and videography skills, ensuring that you capture stunning images and videos. Embrace the camera's capabilities, experiment with different settings, and continually refine your techniques to elevate your creative output.

Recommended Settings for Different Scenarios

The Sony Alpha A7CR/A7C II is versatile, allowing you to adapt settings based on various shooting scenarios. Here are recommended settings tailored for different situations to help you capture the best images and videos.

1. Portrait Photography

- **Shooting Mode**: Aperture Priority (A)
- **Aperture**: f/1.8 to f/2.8 (for shallow depth of field)

- **Shutter Speed**: Auto (let the camera adjust)
- **ISO**: 100-400 (adjust according to light conditions)
- **Focus Mode**: Eye AF (to ensure focus on the subject's eyes)
- **White Balance**: Daylight or Cloudy (for natural skin tones)
- **Picture Profile**: Standard or Portrait (for pleasing skin tones)

2. Landscape Photography

- **Shooting Mode**: Aperture Priority (A)
- **Aperture**: f/8 to f/16 (for deep depth of field)
- **Shutter Speed**: Auto (use a tripod for stability)
- **ISO**: 100 (to minimize noise)
- **Focus Mode**: Single AF (focus on a specific point, typically one-third into the scene)
- **White Balance**: Daylight or Custom (depending on the time of day)
- **Picture Profile**: Landscape (for vivid colours)

3. Action and Sports Photography

- **Shooting Mode**: Shutter Priority (S)
- **Shutter Speed**: 1/500 sec or faster (to freeze motion)
- **Aperture**: Wide open (f/2.8 to f/4) for faster shutter speed
- **ISO**: 400-1600 (adjust based on lighting conditions)
- **Focus Mode**: Continuous AF (for tracking moving subjects)
- **Drive Mode**: Continuous Shooting (to capture multiple frames)
- **White Balance**: Auto (or set according to lighting)

4. Night and Low-Light Photography

- **Shooting Mode**: Manual (M)
- **Aperture**: Wide open (f/1.4 to f/2.8)
- **Shutter Speed**: 1/30 sec or slower (use a tripod)
- **ISO**: 800-3200 (increase as needed)
- **Focus Mode**: Manual Focus (to achieve precise focus in low light)
- **White Balance**: Auto or Tungsten (for warm light sources)
- **Picture Profile**: Standard (for natural colours)

5. Macro Photography

- **Shooting Mode**: Aperture Priority (A)
- **Aperture**: f/2.8 to f/5.6 (to achieve a balance between depth of field and sharpness)
- **Shutter Speed**: Auto (use a tripod for stability)
- **ISO**: 100-400 (to reduce noise)
- **Focus Mode**: Manual Focus (for precision)
- **White Balance**: Custom (to match lighting)
- **Picture Profile**: Neutral (for better post-processing)

6. Video Recording

- **Shooting Mode**: Manual (M)
- **Frame Rate**: 24p or 30p (for cinematic look)
- **Shutter Speed**: 1/50 sec (double the frame rate rule)
- **Aperture**: f/4 to f/8 (to keep the subject in focus)
- **ISO**: 100-800 (adjust based on lighting)
- **Focus Mode**: Continuous AF (for tracking moving subjects)
- **White Balance**: Custom or Daylight (to maintain colour consistency)
- **Picture Profile**: S-Log3 (for better dynamic range in post-production)

By using these recommended settings for various scenarios with the Sony Alpha A7CR/A7C II, you can optimize your camera's performance and capture stunning images and videos in any situation. Always remember to adapt settings based on specific conditions and personal creative preferences to achieve the desired results. Happy shooting!

THANK YOU FOR READING

www.ingramcontent.com/pod-product-compliance
Lightning Source LLC
Chambersburg PA
CBHW062111220526
45471CB00010B/3690